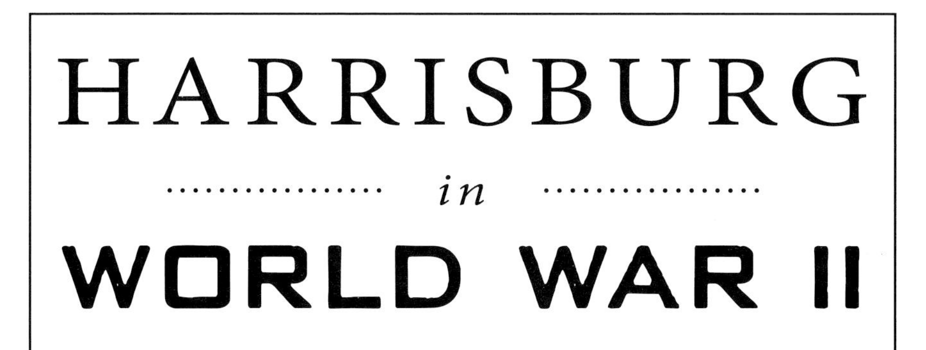

# HARRISBURG *in* WORLD WAR II

Rodney Ross

Published by The History Press
Charleston, SC
www.historypress.com



*Back cover, bottom*: V-J Day celebrated on Market Square. *From the* Evening News. *Courtesy of PennLive.*

First published 2021

Manufactured in the United States

ISBN 9781467147590

Library of Congress Control Number: 2021934140

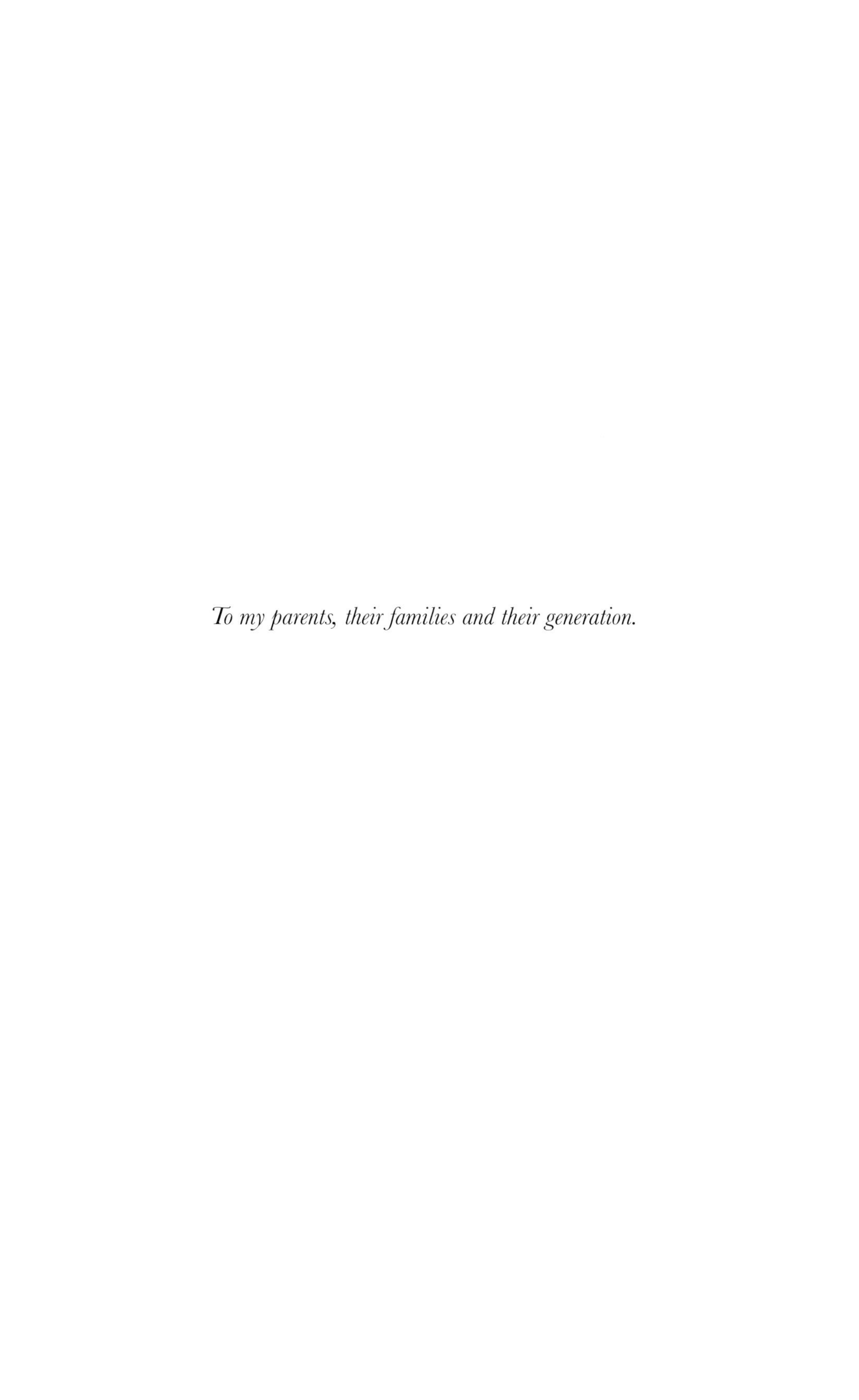

*To my parents, their families and their generation.*

# CONTENTS

# PREFACE

Books about Harrisburg are few and specialized, in some instances pictorials, without narration and bibliography. No period studies exist.

*Harrisburg in World War II* fills a void, chronicling a homefront experience. The work contains nine chapters, each possessing an integrity yet tied to a sequence. My discoveries of the wartime city brought forth revelations.

Harrisburg's defensive mobilization is recalled. Municipal offices, churches, schools, clubs, hotels and industries side by side the USOs, the YMCA and the YWCA did their bit. Citizens enlisted for bond, Red Cross, scrap, foreign aid and blood drives. Hollywood sent stars for promotions.

Newspapers contributed public service as well as news, cartoons, advisory columns, movie reviews, comic strips, letters and war-referenced advertisements. I have devoted attention to mustered downtown theaters and popular music.

Federal programs required teamwork. For the most part, local officials cooperated with conscription, internal security, civil defense, rationing and public health.

The Harrisburg military district harbored military bases and war industries, drawing service personnel and migrant labor. The influx aggravated housing, traffic, crime and vice. Authorities had their hands full.

Wartime challenged the status quo. Contemporaries questioned river bridge tolls and Sunday movie bans.

I researched newspapers and secondary sources. Remarks of locals add spice.

I hope this is a beginning. There are untapped materials to be mined and many tales to be told about the city on the Susquehanna.

# ACKNOWLEDGEMENTS

I am indebted to many for their help.

The Dauphin County Library provided relevant information and online newspapers.

David J. Morrison of the Historic Harrisburg Association graciously accessed his organization's materials.

Ken Frew and his colleagues at the Historical Society of Dauphin County answered inquiries.

Joe Hermitt at *PennLive* accommodated reprint requests.

The guidance and patience of Banks Smither and Crystal Murray at The History Press were greatly appreciated. The Press's Brittain Phillips taught me marketing tips.

Donna Jane Tardy shared recollections of wartime travel.

James R. Zeiters imparted remembrances and pictures.

Nick and Susan Bianchi tendered insights about Italian Americans.

I thank Kathleen Zehner for her interest and support.

My late parents left behind photographs, books, newspaper clippings and other invaluable memorabilia.

A standing O goes to my wife, Aida, for putting up with my self-imposed solitude and preoccupation.

*Harrisburg in World War II* is really a joint enterprise. The work could not have been completed without my daughter Christine's typing, editing, graphic and computer skills.

# 1

# BLUE DECEMBER

## 1941

Japan's December 7, 1941 attack on Pearl Harbor surprised and enraged Harrisburg. In response to an unforeseen emergency, the city mobilized and readied itself. Both public and private agencies marshalled resources for a four-year endeavor.

Once war broke out, the United States War Department warned of industrial sabotage. Mayor Howard E. Milliken, Harrisburg Defense Council chairman, alerted auxiliary police and firefighting stations. He told residents to abide by emergency declarations. Milliken promised federal authorities assistance: "We will co-ordinate all efforts in line with instructions from Washington." Officials posted guards at rail bridges crossing the Susquehanna River. The Central Iron and Steel Company and the Harrisburg Steel Corporation likewise assigned sentinels, as did the Pennsylvania Power and Light Company (PPL).

Suspicious noncitizens were accounted for quickly with the Federal Bureau of Investigation's (FBI) cooperation. Authorities arrested and investigated Kumeji Deguchi, a Japanese national in town to entertain at a café. The U.S. Department of Justice required all Nipponese people to stay at home and asked locals as well as state officers to apprehend on appearance those out of doors or in gatherings. Following the regulation, Harrisburg police and FBI agents seized eight German and Rumanian nationals, and Chief of Police Oscar Blough revealed the presence of three Japanese long-term U.S. residents. Additionally, a state police flying squadron, one of the Pennsylvania units organized to cope with local threats and parachute raids, deployed to the city.

Two children admire their protector by a Harrisburg bridge. *Photograph by Julia Comstock Smith from the* Evening News. *Courtesy of PennLive.*

Harrisburg's air defense became a priority. The Riverside Fire Company's siren, all city fire bells and industrial plants' whistles would signal a raid. The enemy's approach would be communicated to local headquarters from observers outside the town. Deputy wardens, operating with the city's sixty-one districts, would shelter citizens, locate gas explosives plus collapsed power lines and pinpoint fractured gas mains as well as severed water lines. They would minister to casualties, guard against burning home lights and give notice of incendiary projectiles. Officials requested station wagon donations to be presented at 211 Locust Street, the Defense Council Headquarters, needed to serve as medical vehicles and personnel carriers. Chief Blough circulated a catalog of "dos and don'ts" during air assaults. On December 12, defense authorities scheduled courses for raid wardens.

On December 16, a call requested volunteers to staff the air raid warning system. Harrisburg's Aircraft Filter Center processed all messages of oncoming aircraft and operated twenty-four hours hours. Officials welcomed women signees at Locust Street.

As a public service, the *Harrisburg Telegraph* told residents how to respond if the enemy struck: "Keep Under Cover; If Outdoors, Lie Flat; Leave Car or Bus; Turn Off Gas Connection; Avoid Top, Street Floors; Open Windows Partially; Put Out, Conceal Lights; Be Calm, Avoid Panic." "Clip this out, keep it handy," the notice urged.

Blough complained that parked cars on city streets hindered air defense. Charging owners with an unwillingness to pitch in during wartime, he warned vehicles afford the "best aids the enemy has during air raids." Moisture from cars gleamed from random illumination and disclosed locations, he contended, and cars on streets indicated bridges and other defenseless targets. Besides, parking throughout the night hampered the movement of emergency and military vehicles as well as firefighting equipment.

Officials cautioned corporations of the air threat. Conferees representing Swift and Company, Central Iron and Steel, Telegraph Press, McFarland Printery, Harrisburg Gas, United Ice and Coal, along with the Pennsylvania Railroad (PRR) and the Harrisburger Hotel assembled with Blough to develop defense. Moreover, Mayor Milliken told a Shine Luncheon Club that measures to take during a bombing would be published in the press and circulated in a pamphlet.

Media lent cooperation. WHP radio stopped broadcasting weather information about winds, barometric readings or anything else that might aid the enemy. Similarly, Dr. Ray Heverling, an optometrist, discontinued daily weather forecasting with a *Telegraph* ad until the war's end, expressing regret to readers but assuring customers they could still receive professional, inexpensive glass service.

Downtown stores initiated air raid precautions. Bowman's on Market Street proclaimed "lights out evenings," closing before 6:00 p.m., claiming better service and benefits for employees, such as more free time for relaxation and self-enjoyment. The management anticipated better work performed the next day. Sears Roebuck and Company on Market Square bragged about its blackout drill carried out with flying colors. Blumenstine Electric, a Third Street retailer, offered blackout lamps among its fifteen thousand commodities, directing, "If You Can't Find It Elsewhere Go to Blumenstine Electric."

One neighborhood studied a proposal to protect residents. In north Harrisburg, citizens conferred in Saint Mark's Methodist Church to discuss building a bomb shelter. The idea started when thirty people talked about the plan in a private home. But Arnuad C. Marts, head of the Pennsylvania State Council of Civilian Defense, stifled the project, saying it would turn aside resources from real requirements.

Suspicions about enemy aliens fed fears about espionage and sabotage. Harrisburg acted to counter alleged threats. Commensurate to posting sentries at bridges and plants, the city forbid car parking under bridges. The ban applied to subways on Market and Herr Streets. Authorities blocked off the State Street Bridge, adjacent to the Harrisburg Steel Corporation. Vehicles moving northward on Tenth Street used the Paxton Creek Bridge to Cameron Street. When questioned about safeguarding municipal waterworks, local defense coordinator John B. Warden confirmed their protection. He said Reservoir Park, site of a water supply, remained off limits and asked residents to stay out. But he believed, despite the regulation, that citizens could access the park for winter recreation.

Cartoons and comic strips reinforced anxieties about domestic enemies. Frank Finsley's *Yankee Doodle* referenced spying and sabotage while demeaning "sneaking fifth column rats gnawing away at the country's foundation" and questioned "when is America going to wake up." Norman Marsh's *Dan Dunn* predicted, "The invasion will be from within and without!!" while *Thimble Theater* mentioned "getting rid of spies" and Ham Fisher's *Joe Palooka* scripted "Nazi spy."

A renowned columnist confirmed the scare. Dorothy Thompson claimed, "Axis Agents Still Operate."

Pearl Harbor reinforced a racially tinged image of uncivilized and subhuman Japanese. Accused of treachery for attacks without declaring

The Japanese cobra, treacherous and infamous. *From the* Evening News. *Courtesy of PennLive.*

hostilities while conducting diplomatic negotiations, they fell victim to name-calling with a slur like "Jap" and received tags such as "Little Brown Men" or "Little Yellow Men" invading the Philippines. A First World War veteran volunteered to oppose the Japanese: "When the Japs took a sneak punch I couldn't stand it. No honorable nation attacks before a declaration of war." Harrisburg columnist Nobe Frank debased "The Japs—More yellow than shows in their skins." An army officer in the Philippines judged Japanese soldiers contemptible and boasted that an American offensive would put the enemy to flight into the ocean.

They were editorialized as "deceitful," "vicious" and "inhumane" for causing war and attacking Americans, as correspondent Dewitt Mackenzie demonized Japan's soldiery as racial fanatics, branding the country "pagan" and "barbaric." WHP's *We, the People* aired an exposé concerning the mysterious Black Dragon Society, supposedly enshrined to govern Nippon with overbearing power.

The year 1941 would be recalled as when the Western Hemisphere versified the motto, "Remember Pearl Harbor." To further resentment, a forty-year-old dentist composed "We'll Show Those Japs That They're Saps," a ditty promising revenge.

Harrisburg intensified disfavor for all things Japanese. A Swatara Township assessor, puzzled because his ink eraser stopped functioning after five years of reliable use, on examination observed "Made in Japan." "That's just like the Japanese," he exclaimed, "going bad without a moment's notice." The G.C. Murphy Company Five and Ten Cent store at 215 Market Street removed all Japanese-made goods, ordering their transfer in a way that would prohibit purchase. The Zembo Mosque's Japanese trees became cherry.

A few uttered disbelief. Mrs. George Shillinger of North Fourteenth Street saw Nazi Germany's complicity at work and believed Japan planned to dominate Asia. Yet, she theorized Pearl Harbor represented Tokyo's desire to disengage from China. With twenty-one years of missionary experience in Nippon, she refused to accept such an attack could take place. Mrs. Shillinger had departed Japan six months before, and she and her husband had dismissed the possibility of war.

Meanwhile, newspapers glorified Filipinos' heroic resistance to Japanese invaders. A Philippine resident demonstrated concern about the fate of his relatives in the islands and his own safety in Harrisburg. Fearing Japanese identification, he wore a button of red and white, setting him apart as a Filipino.

The Zembo Mosque renamed its Japanese trees "cherry" after Pearl Harbor. *Photograph by Christine L.G. Ross.*

Harrisburgers' stereotyping and racism extended beyond Asians. In a war to defend democratic freedoms, the city exhibited racial prejudice and discrimination against Black people. Classified ads drew a color line on hiring:

"A white girl or woman—general housework. Help with 2 children. Sleep in"
"Girl—white—Regular or part time schoolgirl. Housework in apartment"
"White girl—for general housework."
"Wanted—White girl or woman."
"Wanted—Second cook. White [male]."
"Store room clerk—Experienced white."
"Wanted—experienced cook, white, sleep in, colored sleep out [female]"
"Housekeeper—White, over 40."
"Experienced white waitresses"
"Wanted—White men for waiters, store room and beverage work…Penn Harris Hotel."

The comic strip *Boots* pictured a Black female servant speaking African American Vernacular English as overweight with large lips and bulging eyes and wearing a kerchief beside a Caucasian woman drawn as blond, well-built and sexy. Newspapers headlined alleged Black crimes as "Negro," suggesting lawbreaking and immoral behavior as inbred traits.

De facto racial segregation prevailed in the city. The Black Phyllis Wheatley Branch of the Young Women's Christian Association (YWCA) established a United Service Organizations (USO) unit and a Civilian Defense Committee. It planned a dance for Black troops at the Indiantown Gap Military Reservation located east of Harrisburg.

War's advent animated area industries and commercial enterprises. The federal Office of Production Management's (OPM) contracting unit held an exhibit of products required by the military at the Reading Company's rail yards, a visit of eight hours. Discussions ensued to conclude war contracts. The Central Iron and Steel Company revealed agreements. The 1942 Building Show announced displays would promote the theme "build, repair, and remodel for defense." A three-day gathering of the Associated Pennsylvania Constructors in the Penn Harris Hotel promised manpower and assets for defense. Moreover, insurance agencies envisioned a new market and included war-provisioned policies.

On December 11, workers' unions representing the American Federation of Labor, the Congress of Industrial Organizations, railroads and others set up the United Labor Committee for American Victory. Members affirmed determination to raise production and unite to maintain America's defensive stride. The International Garment Workers' Michael Johnson tendered help to Mayor Milliken, making known that "we are pledged to do everything within our power to bring about victory for American arms." Likewise, the board of trustees at the North Street Union Labor Hall approved defense bond purchases. The Carpenters' Local Union, Number 287, on Locust Street, promised to make an investment.

Retailers and utilities pledged support for the war, abetted by self-promotion. Sutliff Chevrolet on South Cameron Street marketed trucks "For Total Defense Effort." The Automatic Stoker Sales Company on Derry Street urged purchase of the Iron Fireman, a furnace, to conserve fuel and cut costs, claiming it a major aid to defense. Eversharp featured a pen and pencil set for servicemen, styled with a clip facilitating deep pockets. To ready for victory gardens, Schell's Seed Store on Market Street thought tilling instruments would be the favored Christmas presents. The PPL publicized its readiness to serve and proclaimed, "IT IS ALL OUT FOR

AMERICA NOW." The Bell Telephone Company's regulations attempted to discourage unessential calls.

Wartime failed to dampen enthusiasm for the annual Farm Show. Livestock and chicken entrants surpassed the previous year.

Pearl Harbor energized Harrisburg's Red Cross. The canvass for the Red Cross War Fund goal started on December 15. Eight days later, reports placed the drive under its target. Donations came from unexpected sources: a young convict, barred from military service and defense employment, sacrificed twelve-dollar savings, and a Japanese resident contributed an anonymous thirty-dollar gift. To release full-time nurses for war duty, the Red Cross began the Volunteer Nurses' Aid program in city hall. The Jewish Community Center (JCC) provided a supplemental home nursing course. The Red Cross chapter gave yarn to female employees of the Bureau of Employment and Unemployment Compensation to knit bed coverings for military personnel.

Publicity engulfed the Red Cross's "blitzkrieg" crusade. Its poster proclaimed, "Your Red Cross Needs You!" Radio and Hollywood helped. Celebrities performed a sixty-minute benefit over WKBO on Christmas Eve.

Charitable organizations expanded services. The Salvation Army's advisory board promised a salvage campaign. Christmas Seals pledged its collected moneys to health improvement and tuberculosis management. "War and tuberculosis are deadly allies," remarked Dr. C.R. Phillips. On December 17, the Tuberculosis and Health Society of Harrisburg and Dauphin County extended total resources to the United States Public Health Service to maintain national well-being.

Wholehearted support came from civic groups. The Harrisburg Chamber of Commerce took note of a national broadcast from the president of its country-wide organization regarding "The Duty of Business in War." The city branch promised the parent body to commit its "staff to do our full share...even to suspension of other activities." Perceiving national defense as primary, the chamber vowed to go all out. Members endorsed the air corps' Civilian Pilot Training Program. They pledged information for businesses and consumers.

Other civic-minded bodies contributed. The Motor Club of Harrisburg outlined precautions for an air raid, assuming the city could come under attack because of proximity to defense installations. The Quota Club affirmed backing for the Red Cross drive, and the Business and Professional Women's Club gave a twenty-five-dollar donation. The Kiwanis Club prepared a slate of programs for young people.

The Harrisburg Junior Chamber of Commerce offering flight training facts. Mary Louise Adams and Jane Hollister staff the booth. *From the* Evening News. *Courtesy of PennLive.*

Fraternal and sororal societies helped. On December 8, the Capital City Lodge, Number 12, Fraternal Order of Police, elected to purchase defense bonds to the value of $5,000. Harrisburg's USO centers planned activities for the December 20–21 weekend, partly to greet men of the Twenty-Eighth Division, lately arrived from southern training. Dinner invitations, midget auto competitions and dances hailed their return. The YWCA on Fourth and Walnut Streets held a Welcome Home Dance, asking local girls to act as junior hostesses.

The servicemen's spiritual comfort received attention. The Young Men's Christian Association (YMCA) scheduled worship, coinciding with an announcement by President Franklin D. Roosevelt. The prayer periods took place on New Year's Day.

Veterans did their bit. To aid the city, the American Legion, Harrisburg Post Number 27, volunteered as auxiliary police and air raid wardens. It purchased "special equipment" and bonds. The H.L. Calder Post, Number 31, Veterans of Foreign Wars, created defense committees, and Company

D, Eighth Regiment, Veterans Association, made a Red Cross donation and a bond acquisition.

The clergy pitched in. Preceding Pearl Harbor, war-related messages issued from podiums. An ad for a December 7 discourse by Bruce P. Gernet asked, "What Will Stop Hitler's Mad Rush to World Power?" In the Education Building's Forum, the Right Reverend Monsignor Fulton J. Sheen lectured help for Russia's population should exclude support for communism. Every other week the National Catholic Community Service of the USO sponsored dances for servicemen at its North Street center. Pastors occasionally sermonized on war-affected themes, and one church invited soldiers for a supper. Once war began, a former Japanese missionary spoke to the Christ Lutheran Church about Japan's Christian Church and Tokyo's aggression.

Youngsters and schools espoused patriotism. Newspaper carriers brought war stamps to patrons' doors for sale. The Harrisburg Area Council of Boy Scouts, composed of thirty-five city units, helped. Senior Girl Scouts fed sentries at city bridges. Harrisburg's Girl Scout Council considered medical and nutritional programs. Public schools piped in

The Education Building's Forum on Walnut Street, site of wartime programs. *Photograph by Christine L.G. Ross.*

President Roosevelt's radioed war proclamation, followed by the National Anthem. John Harris High School students heard a Bill of Rights address and flag-waving music. The program included the Pledge of Allegiance. Uptown, William Penn High organized a Junior Red Cross. Camp Curtin Junior High formed a model airplane club. Curtin also raised money for the Red Cross. On December 20, the district superintendent announced a system of air raid drills.

Parents and schools cooperated. The Hamilton Parent Teacher Association learned of air raid exercises on December 17. Its sister organization at Cameron established aims and means for bond raising.

Harrisburgers rushed to the colors. Recruiting stations were "jammed" and "flooded." Recruiters rejected underaged boys and a British subject. A World War I veteran, accused of disorderly behavior, had his jail time set aside on a pledge to sign up. The enlistment scurry dropped off, and by late December, military officers spoke of a recruitment campaign. Yet, Harrisburg sign-ups for the army reached 4,744 in 1941. Between December 14 and 20, the Third Corps area, which included the city, occupied top spot for the country's enrollments.

Pro-Allied and international sentiments held sway. A British Trade Mission representative spoke of "Britain's War Effort" at the YMCA. The comic strip *Pam* by A.W. Brewerten referred to an English secret mission. In paperback, *The Battle of Britain*, based on the British Air Ministry's documents and "dedicated to those great flyers, the R.A.F.," sold for twenty-five cents. Market Street's Colonial theater ran *Confirm or Deny*, a picture demonstrating teamwork between Americans and Britons in wartime London. In the Penn Harris on December 14, the Carpathian-Russian Council adhered "to the defense of America and the liberation of the Slavic nations from the tyranny of Hitler." A literary critic reviewed favorably *Mission to Moscow* by Joseph E. Davies, a pro-Soviet publication. An evangelist, back from Asia, told the Women's Missionary Society of the Fourth Reform Church of heroic actions by the Republic of China against the Japanese invaders. The Mary Sachs Store on Third Street welcomed a unique exhibition and merchandising of China's goods. A fraternity of Italians, the Lodge Carlo Alberto, Order of the Sons of Italy, disassociated itself from Rome's fascist regime, embraced a pledge to the United States and added a bond purchase and a Red Cross donation. The State's theater staged *South American Nites* on December 29, featuring "That Latin Heat Wave" with attractive women hoofing to Latin rhythm. Furthermore, newspapers accommodated a global perspective with maps accompanying war reports.

*Top*: Harrisburg youths in the Market Street recruiting office hurry to enlist. *Photograph by Ensminger Studio from the* Harrisburg Telegraph. *Courtesy of PennLive.*

*Bottom*: Recruits marching down Market Street on their way to the New Cumberland Army Reception Center. *Photograph by Ensminger Studio from the* Harrisburg Telegraph. *Courtesy of PennLive.*

Red Cross volunteers rally thumbs up for victory at the Penn Harris Hotel. *From the* Evening News. *Courtesy of PennLive.*

Residents identified with love of country symbols. A photograph of women with a thumbs up signaled victory. Ann Sheridan, an actress, donned a "V for Victory" hairstyle in the film *The Man Who Came to Dinner*. The movie *They Died with Their Boots On* glorified George Armstrong Custer. The minute man image graced press advertisements. Radio and observances celebrated the 150-year anniversary of the Bill of Rights. Undisputed reverence greeted the flag of the nation. Legion Post 27 requested membership to show the banner every day at houses and businesses. The veterans pressed Harrisburgers to do the same and instructed on elevating and lowering. The Pennsylvania Railroad yards raised an oversized flag in an awe-inspiring ritual. Bowman's advertised the flag in varied sizes as "a symbol of democracy for the whole wide world!" When a busboy mouthed offensive comments during the playing of the National Anthem, he came in for disorderly conduct charges and incarceration.

Scam artists exploited wartime. Blough urged awareness of persons posing as collectors for the national emergency, as city hall had not authorized such a right. His warning came too late for a young woman on Seventeenth Street who surrendered antique dishes.

A letter to the *Evening News* regarded soldierly welfare. The correspondent warned that men in military installations risked drink and female temptations. The writer endorsed spirits' prohibition inside encampments.

Old Glory. *Author's collection.*

War's advent found Harrisburg air minded. The Chamber of Commerce enacted the Civilian Pilot Training Program at the Harrisburg Academy, a preparation for air force candidates. Private pilots organized for defense. The Harrisburg Lodge of Elks set up the Air Corps Institute to ready trainees for examinations, with instruction given by teachers in public schools. Complementary to the aeronautic mood, the Senate theater on Market Square screened Bud Abbott and Lou Costello in *Keep 'Em Flying*, a comedy about air corps training with a final musical score presenting airmen singing and planes in flyover *V* patterns. In 1941, "keep them flying" became a patriotic idiom.

Late December saw the populace acclimatized to wartime. Crossword puzzles and bridge remained popular. War toys enthralled children. A sports-crazy town continued athletics, being necessary for morale and diversion. Boxing entertained, and soldiers' matches found sponsors and patrons. The *Telegraph*'s outdoors editor, Michael Seaman, mused how the war might affect hunting and fishing. Despite the ominous backdrop, yuletide shoppers crowded stores.

Newspapers differed on the popular mood. The *Evening News* pronounced it "merry." But the *Telegraph* detected a "somber" frame of mind tempered by war's work pace and families without sons.

Perhaps the *Harrisburg Sunday Courier* prognosticated best. Its editorial "Let's Take Things as They Come" anticipated change and abnegation:

> *Life is going to be different for us....It's the war.*
> *Self-denial and sacrifice will be necessary for each one of us. First of all we must think og* [sic] *the needs of the nation and our ability to make personal contributions of whatever sort are necessary.*

2

# SUMMONS TO DEFENSE

## January 1942–June 1942

Pearl Harbor aroused a flurry. Harrisburgers had been assigned to Hawaiian and Philippine outstations. With Pacific possessions under attack, relatives and friends pushed for news.

Local draft boards hastened call-ups. Officials considered recalling those twenty-eight and older. The army took married registrants.

Steel plants ran throughout the week. The Harrisburg Steel Corporation, with both naval and army obligations, had operated on a seven-day basis. The Central Iron and Steel Company followed suit.

The city prioritized air defense, but alerts encountered snags. Officials considered silencing police, fire and ambulatory vehicles so that sirens only announced an alarm and then dropped the scheme. They likewise decided against firehouse bells because of metal scarcity. They finally agreed to purchase enough sirens so that warnings could be heard throughout. Also, finding sufficient pumpers, hoses and first aid cots became an urgency.

Appeals called for volunteers. The municipality placed police on emergency call. Mounted patrolmen reported for training. Women received encouragement to participate. Answering the summons, the Associated Aid Society and the Girl Scout leadership embraced air defense instruction. By spring, thousands enlisted to serve.

Officials selected shelters. Luminous signs identified them. They picked sturdy buildings of abundant area in the downtown: the Grayco Apartments, the YWCA, the Pomeroy's and Feller stores, the Sears Roebuck retailer and the Blackstone as well as Market Square structures. Six edifices in

City hall seen sandbagged, looking north along Aberdeen Street. *From the* Evening News. *Courtesy of PennLive.*

the capitol complex rounded out the selections. Later additions included the Penn Harris and Harrisburger Hotels; the Odd Fellows Building; the Keystone Warehouse; the Doutrich store; the State Street Building; the Gannett, Eastman and Fleming Building; the YMCA; and the Payne-Shoemaker Building.

The emergency sparked precautions. Officials sandbagged city hall. They readied plumbers to repair water mains. They used fingerprinting and identification tags for casualties. The county prison required protection. Zoo animals would be shot out of fear an air raid would uncage them and endanger the public. Later, the municipality reconsidered, contemplating their transfer to a Susquehanna River island.

Great Britain's blitz experience benefited Harrisburg. The city modeled its air warning center on England's. William Penn High and firefighters viewed British films. Officials demonstrated incendiary dousing. They distributed sand. Two women complained of too small an allotment for the burial of two persons, not realizing the sand's use for extinguishing firebombs.

Blackout stipulations pertained. Newspapers published regulations as a public service. Rules barred lights from buildings during tests, and violators risked fines or jailing. At first, dimmers blocked traffic lights, but accidents caused their replacements by rheostats. Officials ordered boats off the Susquehanna. Initially, all theaters closed, and the Harrisburg City Library promised to do so. Hospitals conducted drills.

Blackouts occurred on May 20 and June 23, and defense officials judged them successes.

Advice poured forth. Telephone use had to wait, and calls could be made one hour after an all clear. Time could be passed with luminous cards and games. Streets had to be vacated. Authorities advised about fractured water mains and firebombs. Based on Britain's example, they suggested a family refuge room containing a wooden overhang for underneath protection. Residents received hints concerning flying glass. Hanging a felt drapery screened illumination and shielded, sucking up windowpane splinters.

Businesses lent self-promotional façades. An ad marketed blackout paint. Another pushed blackout window shades. The term *blackout* spotted eyeglasses. An underwriter offered bomb insurance. The Hotel Bolton plugged a blackout party. Bob Fohl's claimed a bombproof café. Rhea's Pharmacy pledged to stay unclosed. Moreover, H.L. Green pitched a "BLACKOUT ON HIGH PRICES."

Caricatures heeded measures. Cartoons ordered residents to become acquainted with their air raid warden and cautioned about closeness to windows. A drawing scolded a man and woman for dancing while confined to a shelter: "Don't dance or indulge in other vigorous activities" because "exercise increases the consumption of much-needed oxygen and raises the temperature uncomfortably." Comic strips contributed. *Moon Mullins* referred to an air raid shelter. *Homer Hoopee* and *Bringing Up Father* spoke of blackouts. Cognizant of the latter, Walt Disney's Donald Duck sandbagged his front door, ran to a subway entrance for cover and piled sand in his house.

Radio and film messaged the peril. WHP broadcasted methods to neutralize incendiaries and poison gas. The Senate showed the March of Time's *When Air Raids Strike*, extolling England's air defense organization, and the feature *Powder Town*, portraying defense workers and slippery spies. The Rio on Walnut Street screened *Pacific Blackout*, Hollywood's initial offering about the homefront. An ad exploited *Eagle Squadron*, which pictured American volunteers in the Royal Air Force, hoping for air raid service

Lieutenant Donald Ross and family, circa 1938. *Author's collection.*

recruits. Plus, *Mrs. Miniver* lauded the English bravery under attack, a motion picture "every one interested in civilian defense should see."

On March 5, the 104th Cavalry captured objectives in a simulation. Lieutenant Donald Ross's troops guarded sites from imaginary parachutists. The drill suggested external as well as internal threats.

Warnings and incidents minded of subversion. Believing fifth columnists operated, authorities instructed patriots to "TALK LITTLE AND LISTEN MUCH." The city acted when suspected youths, a Puerto Rican and a Korean, lingered by the Market Street Bridge. Officers interrogated both but then freed them. Photographs taken of the span suffered confiscation. Private boats required registration. Officials dismissed complaints about patrol craft agitating animal life while on anti-sabotage duty. When Island Park beach opened, police guarded river bridges, prohibited any parking nearby and enforced an 11:00 p.m. curfew.

City spokesmen spread a fear of fifth columnists. A Presbyterian minister wanted Axis operatives unearthed. A federal agent told the Civic Club that ordinary citizens had slight awareness of the fifth column's extent. He warned of the inadequacy of the espionage statutes. At the Zembo Mosque, the Brotherhood of Railroad Trainmen's leadership admonished fellow workers to be watchful.

Radio, cartoons and movies chimed in. WKBO's *March of Time* revealed the FBI's struggle with fifth columnists. The comic strips *Yankee Doodle*, *Draftie*, *Mickey Finn*, *Joe Palooka*, *Little Annie Rooney*, *Bringing Up Father*, *Dan Dunn* and *Pam* warned about spies and sabotage. Donald Duck chided carefree conversation. Hollywood furnished credulity about the undercover enemy. *Don't Talk*, a two-reeler, cautioned that unguarded words helped foreign agents. *The Bugle Sounds* showed the arrests of saboteurs. *My Favorite Spy* reflected an espionage theme. *All Through the Night* had American hoodlums drub an Axis den.

Suspicions descended on nationals of Axis countries. Authorities required German, Italian and Japanese immigrants to surrender "forbidden items" (guns, shells, explosives and shortwave radios). On April 22, police raided houses, netting banned materials. According to the FBI, the haul contained maps, propaganda, factory photographs and bridge information. The homes also coughed up correspondence, firearms, blades, radios, ammunition and foreign literature. Letters seized from a Japanese family compiled correspondence received from parents over a thirty-four-year period. Police saw photographs and maps of Italian factories and thought the seized data would be of value. Yet, a federal agent conceded most material came from loyal households.

Washington ordered the registration of noncitizens from enemy countries. Identification cards became mandatory, and applications arrived in the city post office. Twenty enemy nationals applied the first day. But by mid-February, merely 10 percent of the 325 resident undocumented immigrants from enemy countries enrolled. Courts could authorize "internment in an American concentration camp," a risk for ignoring registration. Authorities detained a woman for neglecting to enroll.

Precautions restricted naturalization. When two hundred foreigners applied for citizenship, the government stopped the proceedings for Harrisburg's Germans and Italians.

Japanese came under particular scrutiny. *Yankee Doodle* strengthened mistrust by picturing Japanese Americans idling at a marine base and propagandized while visiting Japan. Authorities apprehended two walking over the Market Street Bridge but eventually released them. Investigation proved their legitimate presence as professional sex checkers of newborn chicks. Subsequently, two additional Japanese Americans experienced arrest and freedom once the FBI, again, confirmed their trade as sex checkers.

An educational program by federal and state officials urged public alertness to possible sabotage by denaturalized Axis nationals. Nevertheless, when the United States went to war against Bulgaria, Hungary and Rumania, Harrisburg police neglected citizens of these German allies.

Recruitment picked up. The United States Navy's trailer made area visits. The Rio's *Hello Annapolis* encouraged volunteering. The Colonial theater advertised *To the Shores of Tripoli* as the movie that "makes you want to become a Marine." At the Senate, Lieutenant Jimmy Stewart's *Winning Your Wings* won acclaim as "the slickest recruiting job this side of sign here!" Marines enrolled football hero Manny Weaver.

The draft had problems. The United States Public Health Service announced 1,500 youths, of the initial 60,000 draftees tested in the Third Corps area, received dismissals because of venereal disease. City Draft Board Number One advised deferments would be withheld despite spousal dependency. A local columnist thought those draft dodging through manipulative wardship were "as yellow as the Japanese."

Conscription issues landed in the courts. A grand jury handed down indictments because of address changes and unreturned questionnaire lapses. A Jehovah's Witness preacher filed a petition in federal court seeking immunity because of religious affiliation. He protested the categorization as a "conscientious objector," fearing assignment to a government work camp.

The classification and accompanying labor, he argued, clashed with his sacred agreement to the Almighty.

Downtown theaters honored draftees with send-off ceremonies. Family members and well-wishers attended the State for 164 selectees. A City Board Number One representative asked the men to understand their just cause and the customs of the United States. A pastor prayed, and the honorees received Bibles. Draft officials mustered the inductees. They marched to Market Square behind the Susquehanna Township School band and embarked for the New Cumberland Reception Center. Loew's conducted similar observances for 200 men.

Women willingly volunteered. Forty hastened to the Market Street recruiting center, joining the Women's Auxiliary Army Corps (WAAC). Sign-ups hoped to be admitted to the officers' training at Fort Des Moines. In June, many applied for a mere thirty openings.

Light-hearted farce mirrored the call-up. *Mickey Finn* pictured the character Uncle Phil making known his draft board membership. *Draftee* spoofed army life and identified Japan as the enemy. Columnist Pegge Parker joked, "What happened to the patriotic little worm? He joined the Apple Corps." *Private Snuffy Smith*, a movie spinoff from the *Barney Google and Snuffy Smith* comic strip, portrayed a middle-aged Snuffy wangling himself into infantry service. *True to the Army*, another comedy, introduced the tune "I'm Wacki for Khaki." On WHP, Kate Smith, a popular songstress, reviewed *This Is the Army*, an Irving Berlin production.

City officials administered wartime rationing. Washington established the program for allotment of scarce commodities. Japan's invasion of the East Indies reduced the nation's rubber supply. WHP warned of anticipated difficulties. Tire distribution began on January 5 through board-issued permits. Those providing essential services obtained tire and tube grants. Allowances for February allocated five truck tires and tubes to Olewine Cheese House for wholesale deliveries, two tires and tubes to the Harrisburg Gas Company for a service truck and three car tires to Dr. W. Tyler Douglas Jr., a physician. The next month, City Board Number One released tires to a minister, a coal dealer, a meatpacker and some plumbers. City Board Number Three gave permits to a physician and plasterer while City Board Number Two issued twelve tires and tubes for buses of the Harrisburg Railways Company.

The local Office of Price Administration (OPA) verified tire dealers' accounts and investigated violators. City police urged safeguards against thievery, encouraging use of locked garages in place of nightly street parking.

Automobile owners kept track of tire serial numbers. Despite precautions, tire theft and ration breaches occurred, followed by court action. WHP's *Mr. D.A.* warned about a tire-thieving gang. *Dick Tracy* coined the term "bootleg tires." The Keystone Auto Club pressed for severe measures, extending $100 for the apprehension of any tire crook, labeling them "enemies of a country at war." In fact, tire theft donned the odium "sabotage of national defense."

Businesses curbed deliveries. Dairies stopped special visits and Sabbath drop-offs. Robert H. Graupner, a brewer, limited shipments, and Shoemaker's Sea Food Store inaugurated a new plan. Retailers delivered on alternate days and advised shoppers to purchase only what they could handle, buy with care to avoid returns and render undesired items themselves. Harolds Valeteria Cleaners and Dryers asked patrons to fetch single or small pieces so it could save tires and limit service.

Other restrictions became effective. The Associated Aid Societies checked family visitations. Police disused cruiser cars to serve aldermen's warrants. Firefighters discontinued vehicle parades. The Harrisburg Senators baseball team canceled an out-of-state game, the Williams Grove Speedway shut down and the Gretna Players shelved their season. In May, the War Department requested curbs on "Sunday trips, visits to cousin, and petting parties."

Modifications followed rubber's shortage. Girdle availability worried women. Retreading became popular and aligning promised savings. One shoe retailer pressed customers to buy galoshes at once. Authorities advised slow driving and advocated a forty-mile-per-hour limit. Criticism fell on pupils for car use, and Catholic High discouraged student motoring. Reduced traffic meant greater bus and train reliance. Parking meter receipts dropped. Buses considered fewer stops and halted only as scheduled. To reduce pauses, blacked-out traffic lights came under study. With a smaller number of motorists, auto salesmen feared employment loss.

To some, tire restrictions appeared unreasonable. Officials denied Martin R. Nissly's claim for treks to eastern Pennsylvania for wholesale potatoes. A hearse owner sought a tube, arguing his wagon could carry dead and wounded in a crisis. When City Board Number One withheld new tires from a doctor, he decided against making house calls, upsetting a sick father's daughter.

Harrisburgers accommodated rubber rationing. A steelworker certified to purchase preowned tires instead returned the permit. A patriot patched his tire thirteen times, each repair representing an original American colony. The cartoon *Today Blow for Liberty* encouraged walking to work. Newspapers suggested foot care and strolling to the girdleless, as the exercise would be beneficial. But an editorial promised a synthetic rubber thread would resume girth manufacture, and "there will be few Spreading Sallies or Overlapping Olas." The *Telegraph* experimented with wooden treads on a truck. Dairies anticipated carrying milk by horse. A Chestnut Street family thought of using a horse and buggy for a get-together.

The press lampooned the rubber crunch, attempting comic relief. A "no more tires" lament punchlined, "These are the times that try men's soles." *Little Annie Rooney* mused that mules save tires, and Donald Duck impersonated a Native American medicine man, hoping by ritual to get treads. He also commandeered a child's tire swing to replace a flat and installed blackboard erasers as tires for his automobile.

To offset tanker sinkings in the Atlantic, gasoline rationing began in May. Schools held registration. Sticker classifications portioned allotments. For nonessential motoring, *A* allowed three gallons a week; *B* permitted an additional amount, primarily for workers; *C* grants went to essential motorists; and *X* assigned police and firefighters unlimited quantities. The *T* class gave truckers unrestricted fuel.

Registrars faced problems. Drivers requested few *A* grants and depleted the *B*. Officials found applicants less than truthful. When registration ended, more *B* than *A* requests had been discharged. The number of *X* card issues caught the OPA's attention. The agency reported an indictment.

With gasoline scarce, the undeserved *X* classifications caused complaint, and an editorial criticized the number. The Dauphin County Rationing Board considered listing recipients. A deadline to bring back unlawful *X* and *B* stickers yielded three hundred returns. The city discouraged *X* permits for police and firefighters, ordering them to ride buses to work.

Rationing authorities warned the public. Drivers out of gas and stranded on bridges would get no sympathy and could expect no help.

Thievery and illegalities plagued gas rationing. Crooks siphoned fuel from parked vehicles. Filling stations made unlawful transactions, many exhausting their quotas. Boards exercised oversight of several dealers accused of dispensing over and above allotments. One station attendant reported that sixty-five motorists used incorrect permits.

Radio's *Mr. D.A.* highlighted the lawlessness. One episode dramatized hijackers purloining gasoline.

The city adjusted to scarcity. By mid-May, Sunday traffic lightened. Bus riding swelled. The Harrisburg School Board deleted programs. The Harrisburg Merchants' Committee, under Office of Defense Transportation (ODT) order, announced delivery limits. Breyers Ice Cream complied. The

Gas rationing reduces traffic on the Market Street Bridge. Looking west from Harrisburg. *From the* Evening News. *Courtesy of PennLive.*

Rotary Lodge relocated a site. Seiler schoolgirls biked. A Cumberland County shopper arrived in a horse and buggy. The Hoak Dairy Stables' "Tom" wagoned milk to Allison Hill.

Public service voices advised. Sportsmen should curb fishing trips and tend gardens. Driving by oneself aided the Axis, so be patriotic and carpool. Radio promoted automobile "doubling up." A Food Fair ad urged joint commutes. A whimsical reminder told residents that walking could be done without a vehicle. Editorials advocated slower speeds and mass transit.

West Shore shoppers Frances R. Myers and A.C. Crone travel to Harrisburg in horse and buggy and park on Market Square. *From the* Evening News. *Courtesy of PennLive.*

Ironically, newspapers advertised outings. A seashore trip ad blurbed Cape May, New Jersey, as "a perfect summer vacation." Amusement parks publicized short distances and fuel savings as draws.

Reduced motoring conferred benefits but created annoyances. Amorous parking became a patriotic, gas-saving gesture since a lady's man need not invent a mechanical problem for a premeditated stop. Less gasoline meant a slower pace, which helped friendships develop and improved neighborly relations. Confined residents came to appreciate city diversions. Attendance at the zoo increased. The Susquehanna attracted swimmers, boaters and picnickers. Nevertheless, some complained that more walking troubled feet and less gas distanced lovers' lanes.

Humor trailed the gas shortage. A joke on buying fuel teased motorists, telling them to refuse "fill 'er up?" Donald Duck installed pedals beneath his automobile.

Sugar rationing became necessary, as reduced Philippine and Caribbean shipments caused a shortage. Dealers took precautions. Soft drink distributors limited supplies to retailers, did away with quart bottles and adapted to reduced-sized receptacles. The Harrisburg Coca-Cola Bottling Works apologized for lower output but promised the drink retained its excellence. In February, restaurants served sugar only by request. To deter hoarding, merchants restricted purchase. One opinion attributed the shortfall to women buying the sweetener and selling it to acquaintances.

Registration for sugar allocations took place in May. The month before, a WHP broadcast explained the procedure. Teachers and volunteers in schools administered applications. Pupils brought applications home. Any amount of sugar beyond two pounds per household authorities judged as hoarding. Of the 15,831 applicants, 240 already possessed six pounds. Registrars denied them ration booklets. A gag shot photographed Edison Junior High School teachers in fake finger splints and arm slings, purportedly from extreme writers' cramp caused by the demands of registration.

Rationing officials publicized rules for sugar purchases and punishments for their violations. Merchants could sell only to patrons who removed stamps from books in person. Loose stamps without booklets constituted an illegal act. Purchasing with them risked fines and prison time.

Pundits offered pointers on doing without, doing with less and doing with substitutes. In a regular column, Meta Given prescribed coffee without sugar, sugarless quick breads and cream- and honey-coated cereal. She advised resorts to corn syrup, honey and sweet fruits. Juice residue from peach cans produced jelly and fruited buttermilk. Tapioca of mashed peppermint sticks spared sugar. Mrs. Gaynor Maddox, another columnist, promoted

Overstrained Edison Junior High School teachers in finger splints after sugar rationing rush. *From the* Evening News. *Courtesy of PennLive.*

honey, syrups and fruits. She labeled sugar rationing a "blessing to National Health," since the sweetener exemplified an "arch enemy of streamlined and vital figures." Antoinette Donnelly echoed the theme in her column, calling sugary restriction a "beauty boon in disguise" and prompting that "it's good for your figure." She added women might become wise about vitamins too.

Novel recipes appeared. Sara Ann's Cooking Class suggested honey jelly, honey-filled pastries, sugarless applesauce and corn-syrupy hotbreads. A honey and beet mix, borrowed from Russia, saved sugar and fashioned jam.

Housewives demanded sugar for canning and preserving ripened berries and fruits. Extra quotas failed Washington's approval. The state ordered supplements through requests submitted to local boards. To aid canning, the *Evening News* prepared a booklet.

In February, automobile plants stopped assembly lines. Car rationing began. Since new models became limited, buyers needed to meet eligibility requirements. Dealers worried about business, and workers scrambled for transportation. Authorities confined resales to authorized retailers and motorists entering the military. Regulations forbid transfers to friends or family. Vehicles purchased under rationing kept their 1942 standing as "new" once under regulation. In March, city boards released an ambulance and passenger car. They granted the police and a construction superintendent automobiles. Auto permits in May allowed purchases by an electrician, a defense laborer and two corporations. In June, a city board issued three, one going to a nurse.

WHP updated the city on car rationing. Dealers' ads promoted new and used sales to those eligible. M. Brenner and Sons Motor Company's lot held preowned vehicles "for war effort need," and Sutliff Chevrolet on South Cameron Street reminded consumers that "transportation is vital to victory."

Harrisburg entered the national bond drive. Laborers, nurses, firefighters, police, bakers, clubs, ethnic groups, organizations and retailers purchased them. Merchants pushed sales through ads and gimmicks. A furrier claimed a coat acquisition before inflation would pay for itself with bond and stamp savings. Miller's Shoe Store gave free stamps to its 1,000th buyer. At least ten stores established booths. Theaters welcomed buyers.

The municipality took part. A Victory Day Parade followed a canvass requesting pledges. Mayor Milliken selected April 16 as Pledge for Victory Day.

Newspapers augmented support. Editorials backed bond sales. One listed financial and investable advantages. A movie reviewer plugged *To the Shores of Tripoli*, "a film for today, one that'll send you out to buy a few more War

A downtown store displays 1917 and 1942 war bond posters. *From the* Evening News. *Courtesy of PennLive.*

Bonds and Stamps." *Superman*, *Dick Tracy*, *Dickie Dare*, *Draftie*, *Dan Dunn*, *Thimble Theater*, *Brenda Breeze* and *Blonde* joined. In *The Adventures of Patsy*, a character vowed, "I be buying a lot."

Harrisburgers worked victory gardens to offset food shortages. Committees under local defense councils oversaw one thousand plots. The labor produced vegetables, aided nutrition, raised morale and alleviated tension. Radio, slogans ("Food for Freedom" and "Eat What You Can, and Can What You Can't") and comic strips (*Little Annie Rooney*, *Toonerville Folks* and *Tillie the Toiler*) lent endorsement. Press columns specialized in advice, offering guidance about when, how and what to plant. The city supplied free seed, the Garden Club gave a course and children volunteered. The Allison Hill Civic Association developed a plan. Bowman's advertised a garden shop. Schell's Seed Store pushed its gardening wares.

Pests plagued the project. Gardeners coped with beetles and bunnies. Officials recommended box traps and lime to combat rabbit raids. Residents could sympathize with the *Bringing Up Father* character banishing a chicken from his garden.

Industries and businesses took off on a war footing. The Chamber of Commerce facilitated cooperation between local and military officials with heed to the city's industries. In June, it created a group to maintain help for military installations and manufacturers.

Steel companies sped output, expanded plants and operated holidays. *Dr. Christian*, a WHP program, disclosed solutions for accelerated production. The Harrisburg Steel Corporation won the Navy E, the earliest awarded locally. Celebrity broadcaster Lowell Thomas chaired ceremonies at the plant on April 22. Over two thousand employees received E buttons in front of federal, state and local dignitaries. National magazines covered the event. By coincidence, the Senate billed *Joe Smith, American*, which, in addition to a spy theme, applauded defense workers.

Firms received federal contracts at surrounding military posts. *The Nebbs*, a comic strip, cautioned contract overcharges by corporations, an unpatriotic act.

Labor assured cooperation. Loew's theater ran a short subject displaying harmony across government, business and labor. The leader of the Brotherhood of Trainmen advocated loyalty. Edward Miller, representing the Steel Workers' Organizing Committee, affirmed his outfit's patriotism. Attempting to counteract the worker shortage, officials set up training programs for men and women.

Mishaps burdened industry. Despite precautions, accidents took place. A January incident injured three men at Central Iron and Steel. A May fire broke out at Harrisburg Steel.

Non-governmental institutions teemed patriotic. Newspaper ads backed the war, and press employees bought bonds. The Harrisburg Gas Company began food conservation. Aligned with the United States Consumer Program, its "Home Volunteers" campaign offered instruction. Epitomizing the private sector's commitment, *Superman* hailed business and labor teamwork in unfettered capitalism.

The academic year's resumption heightened the schools' wartime activities. William Penn's boys volunteered as couriers and firefighters. They planned a defense dance and formed the Disaster Corps. They also built model airplanes. The school's student body knit for the Red Cross. Many took a first aid course. Students and the American Legion retrieved dated license plates for scrap. "Tag Hitler" became the watchword of the collection. In addition, the school bought war stamps. Its faculty aided draft registration.

The Harrisburg Steel Corporation wins the Navy E. *Courtesy of the Historic Harrisburg Association.*

The Allison Hill high school got involved too. John Harris boys proposed a defense dance, offered firefighter service and made Red Cross stretchers. They debated about the wisdom of military training prior to draft age. The school's girls knitted, studied nutrition and planned a hop. They also collected books for servicemen and gathered supplies for air defense. Pupils recited USO goals in the theatrical performance *We're in the Army* and, in a paean to the nation's Latin allies, enacted a Pan-American playbill. Harris teachers completed a first aid course.

Junior high schools answered the call. Camp Curtin established Junior Red Cross and drafting clubs. Students compiled books for soldiers and collected money for the Cross. They rounded up scrap paper, sold defense stamps and studied home nursing. The school held patriotic programs for bond and stamp purchases as well as George Washington's birthday. Edison, Curtin's counterpart, established a faculty first aid and produced thirty-four afghans.

Elementary schools and their parent-teacher associations complemented the higher grades. Between February and June, Downey pupils bought stamps. Steele's PTA planned Red Cross courses. Melrose's parents supported Red Cross nutrition. They also recruited pupils for a home garden competition. In January, the Harris Park PTA heard a defense presentation.

Private schools expressed the wartime spirit. The Harrisburg Academy debated the appropriate age for military training. In April, it advanced commencement to June 1 to make room for the on-site Air Intelligence School. Catholic High School's PTA sponsored nursing classes and bought knitting yarn. Moreover, it facilitated a talk about World War I martyr Joyce Kilmer and sponsored a discussion about salvage.

By mid-January, the Harrisburg School Board began war readiness. Officials instituted drills, extended defense training, approved debates and endorsed stamp marketing. They mandated two teachers trained in first aid for each school and ratified William Penn's use by the Pennsylvania State College Education Service for defense instruction. State funds financed vocational training. By early April, first aid kits were received by every building. Concerned about war's impact on youth, the district organized a teachers' conference to discuss the ministering of children's adaptation.

The war disturbed school conventions. To meet required defense output, officials considered a two-year high school program to hasten commencement. A drop in attendance occurred as youths enlisted. The district canceled sporting events. Gas rationing disarranged graduation as well as banquet and dance venues.

Black children at Downey Elementary on Calder and Monroe Streets buy war stamps. *Photograph by Ensminger from the* Harrisburg Telegraph. *Courtesy of PennLive.*

By June, Penn students listed graduates serving in the military. The honor roll gave special attention to Nathan Sherman, the first killed.

The school term concluded with ideological themes. The *Pioneer*, John Harris's yearbook, was devoted to a seniors' discussion of "Four Freedoms." William Penn graduates listened to "Sacrifice for Victory" and "Preparation for War" recitations. A speaker before Catholic High graduates said the conflict, rather than safeguarding democracy, represented a clash between totalitarian paganism and Jesus's messages.

Associations sought a public-spirited role. These included the Newcomers Club, the Rotary Club, the Exchange Club, the Kiwanis, the Engineers Society, the Harrisburg Chapter of the War Mothers, the Civic Club, the Women's Club and the Business and Professional Women's Club. They offered services, made donations, discussed morale, entertained military wives, heard talks and viewed war-related films.

Jewish and Italian residents stood at the forefront. The Jewish Community Center gave contributions and informed members. Its films screened Germany's underground movement, America's war summons and Russia's Nazi invaders. In January, the Sons of Italy vowed aid to the United States.

More than servicemen's socials transpired in the YMCA and the YWCA. The men's branch presented a China book review, a *Defense for Victory Show*, a victory garden canning program and a modern industry exhibit. Besides, it met to sponsor support for American prisoners of war. But the emergency forced cancellation of some sports. Its sister arm cooked a ration meal and addressed female employment's effect on housing and industry. It paid attention to refugees in the United States and to those under enemy control. It considered extending aid within Allied borders. In mid-January, Phyllis Wheatley discussed civil defense.

Old soldiers voiced support for the war. The Veterans of Foreign Wars cataloged local industrial and military installations. It placed a full-page ad in the press explaining civilians' duties. The American Legion funded emergency vehicles and saw war films. Strident remarks came from the Disabled American Veterans of the World War. Laurence R. Melton, its commander, exclaimed "Wake Up America" and divulged heartbreak. Accusing the public of shrinking over rationing, being receptive to propaganda and "petty bickering," Melton exhorted men to assume their obligations.

Physical well-being received vigil. The Dauphin County Woman's Christian Temperance Union met in the YWCA's Boyd Hall to discuss "Defend Our Defenders." Conferring in city hall, the Tuberculosis and Health Society of Harrisburg and Dauphin County recognized that mobile populations and housing troubles might facilitate disease. With Harrisburg as a war center, a campaign was necessary to keep the area tuberculosis free.

Benevolent organizations performed a range of activities. The Salvation Army collected paper and recreational furnishings. It gathered sheet music for soldiers. In addition, it funded ambulance and canteen truck purchases. The Red Cross provided nurses aid training and canteen instruction. It sent Russia soap, supplied deployed soldiers kits and mailed U.S. prisoners parcels. It arranged soldiers' voices on recordings from Australia. Besides, the Cross stood ready to furnish emergency aid in response to air attack. It invited blood donations.

Media mirrored voluntary services. Kitty, a *Mickey Finn* character, appeared in a Red Cross outfit, and the funny *Joe Jinks* displayed a sign pleading "Help the Red Cross." WHP aired the Columbia Broadcasting System's dedication to the Red Cross. Also, Loew's showed a short movie on Red Cross creator Clara Barton.

Harrisburgers accommodated service personnel. USOs scheduled dances and activities. By March, seventy-five thousand servicemen had been entertained. At April's outset, the Harrisburg–Dauphin County Defense Council tallied fifteen military post performances, nine dances with dance partners included and over seven hundred women along with fifty-eight

Georgia D. Pickett operates the USO Travelers Aid Service at the Pennsylvania Railroad Station. *From the* Evening News. *Courtesy of PennLive.*

matrons conveyed by uncompensated chauffeuring. In March, more than two hundred servicemen were welcomed in residents' homes. As the volume of soldiers moving in and out of the city picked up, officials established a Travelers Aid Service in June. Later that month, the Reist USO recreational boat tied up by South Street on the Susquehanna.

Harrisburg enlisted in a national book collection for soldiers. The library helped. Loew's exchanged free admissions for books. The Victory Book Campaign set a local quota at fifteen thousand volumes and suggested mailing books to reception centers.

Sundays witnessed soldiers idle and wandering. By law, the city's movie houses remained closed. Theater managers, telephone calls, letters, servicemen and the *Telegraph* endorsed Sabbath motion pictures. Soldiers off duty and on visits found little to occupy their time. One columnist thought films could be spaced between morning and evening worship. A soldier wrote, "I hope the influences that are keeping Sunday movies out of Harrisburg can do plenty about keeping the Japs and Nazis out of the United States." Regardless, the Catholic Center USO on North Street ran Sunday night movies, featuring Henry Fonda in *Young Mr. Lincoln* in mid-March.

Gestures greeted the military. The Dauphin County Courthouse granted soldiers free marriage licenses. A woman paid for a serviceman's meal, saying, "No man in uniform pays when I'm around." The Harrisburg Symphony Orchestra welcomed the military to a free Forum concert. One resident urged motorists to give service personnel rides and recommended a place for their relaxation.

Downtown businesses obliged wants and needs. In April, Bowman's inaugurated East to West Coast picture-taking with stores, enabling soldiers to be photographed for their home folk. The Harrisburger Hotel on Third Street provided rooms for Army Air Corps trainees.

Advice columns offered social pointers. Doris Blake disliked watery-eyed goodbyes and valued unaffected comportment. An "imitation of Niagara Falls" might discomfort, and she believed soldiers prized usable and functional presents. Another writer recommended brownies as the key to correspondence from a military son, promising, "He'll write you 'Thanks a million for the swell cookies.'" Home Institute, a regular feature, explained a serviceman's happiness. Soldiers requested, according to the article, "cigarets [*sic*], candy and Hedy Lamarr....And by 'Hedy Lamarr' of course they meant a visit from the girlfriend." In January, the column reminded readers that soldiers crave letters and had published the *Handbook for a Soldier's Family and Friend.*

A comic strip and motion picture echoed accommodation. *Bringing Up Father*'s character invited a serviceman to his home. Loew's ran *Twin Beds*, scripting an interrupted honeymoon resulting from the bride's dedication to the USO.

The war brought out women. Volunteering became common. Women sewed and knit for the Red Cross. They worked for the air warning service and registered for nursing aides' courses. Ladies manned an auxiliary police detail, promoted bond sales and serviced canteens. Many traveled to Indiantown Gap dances. This concerned a local clergyman, worried about their jeopardizing a sexual good name.

Serving the army attracted some. A former volunteer of World War I's American Expeditionary Force (AEF) sought Christian direction and recreation for the military. Another wrote asking for an upward age for the WAACs. As early as February, a Camel ad had featured a female flight instructor. By May, one hundred had enlisted.

Women took job training and emergency employment. They enrolled in engineering classes conducted by the Pennsylvania State College. They sat for mechanics' programs furnished by the Harrisburg Motor Club and those offered in high school shops. They found an aviation course provided by the Harrisburg School District appealing. Naylor and Goetze, a local firm, tendered women welder instruction. The state approved their hiring. The Central Pennsylvania Business College advertised education for stenographers and spotlighted the "business opportunities for women." The local weather station employed them, inspiring the quip, residents

New employment for women. Hilda Hackenberg (*left*) and Mrs. Phillip Spaid work at the American Oil Company (Amoco) station. *From the* Evening News. *Courtesy of PennLive.*

"will be able to blame the 'weatherwomen' instead of the 'weatherman' for the weather." A newspaper showed the unprecedented: two female employees at their gas station on Front and Verbeke Streets.

Women's entrance into the workforce tampered image and appearance. Grooming and dressing became more scrutinized. The short hairdo vogued. Characterized as a "sleek but feminine coiffure for the service cap," it "easily brushed into a neat and pleasing halo for an alert face." Its acceptance by Hollywood consummated the allure. In addition, actress Alexis Smith tipped on fingernail length and color. For feet, C.B. Rodney's on Walnut Street displayed shoes for Red Cross service, combining "beauty and duty."

Wartime sacrifices little impacted beauty shops. Women demanded their services. Loveliness preserved the spirit, and servicemen had elevated standards. Moreover, women had to pay heed to a more competitive dating market, as the war ousted men from circulation.

Slacks sparked controversy. Women looked "laughable and unflattering," uttered one critic. But slacks were reasonable for defense jobs. They could be worn "with poise and not lose a speck of… feminine attractiveness."

One observer saw no impropriety. Exposure and indecency were not relevant. Rather, pants suited the workplace and the outdoors. He rejected misgivings that the new attire would "make women masculine."

Other styles received commentary. The raised hemline was coined "Pekinese?" for the exposed kneecaps under short petticoats. Entertainer Gracie Allen created the "all-purpose" uniform for every duty. One column applauded women entering unfamiliar occupations in trousers and overalls. Another cited actor Sonny Tuft's belief that the greatest popularity goes to women wearing uniforms. Nevertheless, the artist Tade Styka opined the uniform forfeited femininity.

Material shortages forced women to substitute or forbear. Wooden lipstick tubs conserved metal. Bridal dresses contained less material. Girdles lost stretchable tissue. Cotton and rayon underwear replaced silk and nylon. To give legs the facsimile of stockings, women applied paint. With cosmetic ingredients in limited supply, a columnist recommended olive oil.

Columnists advised mindful contacts with soldiers. One wrote of the "hysteria which uniforms cause," the consequent improper conduct and the degrading impact on girls in general. The column warned of the war's romantic sickness, which she termed "uniformitis," feelings of attraction because of the military garb. Such a tie posed danger for the youths entangled. The columnist criticized dates when picked up and thought wartime marriages needed long courtships.

Actually, the war prompted untraditional dating manners. Another writer believed a woman should share expenses and hint at unpretentious entertainment.

A woman's self-regard received attention. One pundit encouraged walking for exercise and weight control as well as comeliness. Proper diet demonstrated patriotism, "so don't gain weight." To keep fit and attractive while eluding nervousness, a column prescribed "solitaire" and "milk" before turning in. The same writer advised apparel and etiquette guides for socializing. Columnists insisted on beauty and care maintenance for appearance's sake. A letter to the *Telegraph* beseeched women to unite and avoid bickering. Sears Roebuck offered clues on proper posture, claiming it was a "sign of patriotism." Word went to wives to live with their parents in the soldier's absence for his piece of mind.

Dos and don'ts pointed to housewives. The press instructed food conservation and preparation for balanced meals through frugal methods. Single-dish and large-scale cooking received recommendations. Home services and parenting children remained the primary chores. The country's defense centered on a wholesome family and in-house nursing to protect the domicile from bacterium. Warnings poured forth about laxity. Prudence would prevent meat spoilage, restrain water use and avoid excessive stroking when cleaning clothing. Of course, black market collusion was verboten.

Day care needs increased with rises in marriages, births and female employment. In mid-February, the Community Chest and its family council met. An editorial disclosed horrifying reports of child mistreatment and neglect. By March, officials studied the growing urgency.

Communicative mediums summed women's war experiences. Donald Duck mocked women's infatuation with uniforms. *Brenda Breeze* learned car mechanics, and *Thimble Theater* saluted women's determination to serve.

Whistling at female employees sabotages production. *From the* Evening News. *Courtesy of PennLive.*

Loew's ran *Woman of the Year*, a comedy about an "emancipated female." The Senate showed *Joan of Paris*, a drama with a French heroine's namesake aiding resistance to the Nazis. A cartoon warned that distracted machinists whistling at female coworkers might "sabotage" production. WKBO broadcasted a *March of Time* segment, *U.S. Women at War*.

Harrisburg's religious affiliations serviced the war. Sermons elucidated patriotism with appellations like "How to Win the Victory," "Our Duty Toward Our Young Men in Military Service," "Love to God; Love to Country," "Victory Through Christ," "Patriotism Plus" and "Why Does God Allow War?" Pastors cooperated with national synods. The Lutheran World Action aimed to raise $650,000. The Presbyterian's fund campaign enjoyed support. Congregations collected money, held open houses and dined soldiers. They sold defense bonds and stamps, made surgical dressings, facilitated Red Cross blood drives, exhibited military films and dedicated soldiers' service flags. Churches sponsored talks about allies and adversaries.

Ministers had no reservations concerning the war's righteousness. The Market Square Presbyterian Church forewarned of "lethargy" and mandated the edict of a "Spiritual Pearl Harbor." Differences existed about the military training age, yet clerics endorsed common theologies, racism's repudiation, republican government and individual rights. The city's Catholic bishop promised the faithful would shoulder sacrifices and stressed that a victory over hatred should be primary.

Harrisburgers took notice of the nation's neighbors. A cartoon portrayed Uncle Sam protecting Mexico from a menacing Asian person. Radio aired Pan-American themes. A Pan-American Association arose in the city. The Pennsylvania State Museum sponsored a Latin American art show. A YWCA spokesperson applauded the "Good Neighbors of South America." Even home design styled from south of the border became popular.

A warmth existed for Anglo-Saxons. The State theater billed *Captains of the Clouds*, "a stirring saga of the Canadian Royal Air Force," the Loew's *Churchill's Island* praised British defenses and the city scheduled *Eagle Squadron*'s premiere, a Royal Air Force (RAF) tribute. Britain's military personnel visited the area. The Rio screened the English-produced *Target for Tonight* and showed *Canal Zone*, a film demonstrating collaboration between the allies. The British War Relief Society knitted garments for English people. The archbishop of Canterbury and a British pastor aired over WHP. The Colonial ran a lighter rendition of Anglo-American cooperation with *My Favorite Blonde*. Walt Disney pictured Donald Duck and his brood in barrels after donating clothing to Bundles for Britain.

Harrisburg minded China's agony under Japan. The Rotary Club and the Masonic Lodge heard missionaries commiserate with the Chinese. *The Shanghai Gesture*, a Loew's movie, referred to the country's problems, and *Terry and the Pirates*, a comic strip, alluded to its guerrillas. A radio drama by Pearl Buck paid China acclaim. Buck had published *Dragon Seed* in 1941, illuminating Japanese tyranny. The novel received reviews by Rabbi Reuben J. Magil at the Beth El Temple and by a speaker at the YWCA.

Chinese subjects fascinated. A column celebrated the cuisine of "our fighting allies," the "indomitable Chinese," and promoted Fred Wing's *New Chinese Recipes*. A home design article told of a popular "Chinese motif." The *Telegraph* complimented "China's No. 1 man," Chiang Kai-shek.

Harrisburg prized Soviet comradeship notwithstanding its ideology. Books recalled Russia's resistance to outsiders. Eugene Tarle's *Napoleon's Invasion of Russia* and Leo Tolstoy's *War and Peace* drew "parallels." The *Telegraph* reviewed Alexander Werth's *Moscow War Diary*. Rabbi Magil examined Joseph E. Davies's *Mission to Moscow*. At the Colonial, *Our Russian Front* recognized "our great ally." Radio broadcasted Red Army music; one number was called "Song of the Soviet Tankman." Newspapers editorialized favor for the Soviet Union. Residents helped the Red Cross gather aid for the Soviets. Russian food became an item. Russian War Relief promoted the *Russian Cook Book for American Homes*, with profits financing medicines.

Literature heroized underground resistance to Nazi overlords. John Steinbeck's *The Moon Is Down* novelized the "problem of conquering free countries." WHP aired a radio version on the *Kate Smith Hour*. Dorothy Thompson showered praise, distinguishing its "superb propaganda" in spite of a controversial pity for German soldiers. A local column labeled it "this little gem." Another reviewer preferred William Woods's *The Edge of Darkness*, a novel of Norwegian rebellion against Hitler's intrusion.

Radio and film played to resistance. WHP aired a Dutch underground drama. Loew's ran *To Be or Not to Be*, an accolade to Polish freedom fighters.

On June 14, America cheered its allies with United Nations Day. Allied personnel frequented Harrisburg. In April, the Hellenic Orthodox Society feted Greek soldiers. A Norse diplomat spoke before the Executive Club. The city welcomed British airmen in June.

The State ran *The Real Glory*, a reissue of a 1939 production. Unbeknownst to audiences, Philippine president Manuel Quezon protested its rerun because of an unflattering image of his soldiery. Producer Samuel Goldwyn promised to cancel the showings. The *Telegraph* recommended the film and thought it portrayed Filipinos favorably, and the paper praised actor Gary Cooper's performance.

To offset material shortages, Harrisburg launched scrap campaigns. The local Industrial Salvage Committee of the Volunteers of America targeted metals, paper and rags. Retailers gave support and ran ads. Upon conclusion, stores would receive a Salvage for Victory emblem for window display. Market Square's Caplan's collected empty toothpaste and shaving cream containers for tin at two cents per piece. B. Abrams and Sons offered a collector's service. Pabst Blue Ribbon stopped canning. Atlantic gas stations offered to remove dated auto plates without cost. The American Legion announced its last plate collection for April 3. Youths designated Junior Rubber Wardens descended on shoe repair shops to gather worn heels. Women mounted a telephone campaign, dialing five acquaintances who in turn phoned five of their friends. One woman contributed an old vacuum. Car foot pads were donated.

City authorities had media backing. Milliken proclaimed Salvage for Victory week between April 28 and May 4, and WKBO described the effort. The *Evening News* carried Donald Duck gathering scrap in a small car, a two-story fire escape he detached from a building.

Nevertheless, doubters questioned whether can collecting outweighed the gasoline and rubber expenditures it required. Newspapers reported disappointing results.

Conservation accompanied salvage. An editorial advising air raid pointers cautioned to not apply surgical tape to windows or buy a new flashlight if your present one still functioned, as you would save metal. Plumbing care and small radiators economized metals, as would water softeners to avoid congested heater coils. Lawn mower manufacturing ceased on June 30. Stores limited home deliveries as early as January. One wit suggested men convert to bow ties to spare cloth.

Households had a role. Home insulation, coal stokers and kitchen boilers conserved fuel. Cuffless pants preserved materials. Mothers taught daughters how to retain cooking fats and oils.

An editorial titled "Time to Get Serious" scolded for excessive sugar consumption and "aimless knitting." In April, consumers took a pledge, vowing, "I will buy carefully, waste nothing and take good care of the things I have." Comic strips exemplified this. *Joe Jinks* reduced the use of printing inks, and *Little Annie Rooney* substituted whitewash for paint.

The city's youth mobilized. Children sold bonds, bought stamps and gathered scrap. They became Red Cross, civil defense and Salvation Army volunteers and planned a dance as a fundraiser for bond buying.

The Girl Scouts themed a meeting "Volunteers for Victory." Members helped the March of Dimes and the Victory Book Campaign and studied surgical dressing. Brownies wrapped soaps for defense. The Boy Scouts distributed bond literature. Children of Child Welfare Services flag waved on Washington's birthday. They also knitted garments. WHP aired *Youth on Parade*, spelling out the war assistance of the young. *Little Annie Rooney* pictured kids working gardens, applying pesticides and eating beans.

But children required oversight. A columnist rebuked youth for wearing military badges. Another advised mothers to train their daughters in household responsibilities. Speakers harped on wartime obligations. Dr. Garry Cleveland Myers held parents answerable for citizenship education.

Instruct at an early age, he counseled, "to respect the rights and possessions of others."

Symbols saturated Harrisburg, and affection went to the flag. Observances and pageants paid Old Glory homage. Camp Curtin exhibited eighty emblems. The American Legion bought flags for members and pressed for their flying. A letter to a city newspaper wondered why so few residents displayed flags, suggesting the governor order their flying. The press printed guidelines on their proper showing. The East Harrisburg Women's Temperance Union discussed the banner's evolution.

Flag ceremonies became happenings. Milliken designated June 8 to June 14 as Flag Week. An editorial explained Flag Day's significance. Associations and clergy performed rituals. The American Legion Band rendered "The Star-Spangled Banner" at Reservoir Park. At the site, the Reverend Lawrence F. Schott interpreted Old Glory's importance.

"Victory" and "V" appeared as patriotic tags and marks. The tags identified victory soup, victory dinner, victory desserts and victory fruit bread, as well as a Victory Day parade, a Victory Tea, a Victory Book Day and a Pledge for Victory Day. The Capital Bank and Trust Company advertised a safe deposit for Victory. North Second Street's Ference Cheese Shoppe retailed Victory Foods. Hoover's furniture plugged a Victory Home Outfit. The "V" backed nutrition: a "V" campaign for "vittles." It adorned a woman's gown in *Tillie the Toiler* and materialized in a Girl Scouts' recital line. A grooming request asked men to cut their moustaches in the V-form. It labeled the movie *Mister V*. It also aligned singing servicemen in the State's *True to the Army*.

Slogans acknowledged war's arrival. Harrisburgers heard "Americanism Week," "Hale America," "Wake Up, America," "Keep 'em Flying" and "I Am an American Day." The United States Navy published *Remember Pearl Harbor*. Hollywood brought out a film titled the same.

Music, insignia, nomenclature and color expressed love of country. Radio played John Philip Sousa's compositions and the ditty "Keep Mum Chum," a careless talk cautionary. Trainee nurse's aides wore Red Cross defense emblems, filet crochets pictured the American Eagle and the *Evening News* gave away a "MacArthur Victory Badge." Locals thought Italian Lake needed a name change. A couple requested revision of a German-sounding surname. Fashionmongers imitated naval hues and styles. Red, white and blue shone from shoes.

Iconography emanated from film and press. The movie *Saboteur* shot melodrama on the Statue of Liberty. The *Telegraph* ran "Father of Liberty," a paeon to George Washington. The *Evening News* portrayed *Joe Palooka*

A slogan became a movie's title. *From the* Evening News. *Courtesy of PennLive.*

explaining a people's war for democracy and *Little Annie Rooney* articulating America's struggle for freedom. In June, the paper printed excerpts of the Declaration of Independence.

Hollywood abetted Harrisburg's mobilization. Joe E. Brown, Linda Darnell and Deanna Durbin entertained servicemen and encouraged war activities. Gene Raymond, spotted in a Market Street store, arrived on military duty. On radio, Lieutenant James Stewart advanced the air corps and the Andrew Sisters vocalized, a trio said to be "tops with Uncle Sam's men." Not to be forgotten, a North Seventh Street woman composed an ode memorializing Carole Lombard, killed in a plane crash while touring for bonds.

Celebrated servicemen brightened the gloom brought on by battlefield setbacks. Newspapers noticed Sergeant Joseph Lockard's passage through the city. He had given warning of Japanese aircraft nearing Hawaii. For Staff Sergeant Richard M. Cullison's bombing skills, the *Telegraph* editorialized, "The city's pride in its latest hero" who signified "the formidable striking power being mobilized from Harrisburg."

No individual matched the tributes capping General Douglas MacArthur. Newspapers headlined the general without alluding to his men, giving the impression that he engaged the Japanese alone. Radio reported his exploits. A columnist thought a movie appropriate. Another said Market Square should be refashioned "MacArthur Square." Poetry cast him in honor.

The city turned out for holidays. A Memorial Day parade of soldiers and veterans began at Second and Boas Streets and ended at the Harrisburg Cemetery with rites. Independence Day festivities were planned for Reservoir Park. Phrased the "Spirit of '4'," the 104th Cavalry scheduled a military exercise. The USO Council decided to consecrate the Reist recreational boat in unison with the program.

Flying continued to fascinate. Sign-ups increased for private instruction and military training. A columnist offered to raise money for a youth who could not afford piloting lessons. Federal authorities established an aviation school in the Farm Show building to educate mechanics. Public schools offered women similar tutelage. The War Department housed an Army Air Corps (AAC) intelligence school at the Harrisburg Academy. In mid-April, residents learned of Lieutenant Colonel James Doolittle's raid on Japan.

Media galvanized an air power enthusiasm. *Smilin' Jack* mentioned "air maneuvers" and an "advanced air school." It featured accurate and realistic aircraft drawings. Military planes such as the B-17 Flying Fortress and the B-26 Martin Marauder embellished ads. Flyers, it was claimed, preferred Camels.

The interest in flight was encouraged. Milliken announced Aviation Cadet Week. Loew's invited candidates to view *Winning Your Wings*, and veteran pilots attended to speak of their exploits. Press reports and a serial fostered flying. Editorials chimed in, one predicting victory over Germany by way of bombing as soon as 1943. Another thought a family plane might replace the family car.

The war's advent aggravated transportation. Heavy traffic congested thoroughfares, and crowded buses wearied defense workers. The city relocated patrolmen, and police took an FBI traffic program. Buses halted only at designated stops. By July, stores and offices staggered hours. They also wanted residents to walk and to use mass transit.

The war's stepped-up economy increased fumes over the city and hindered smoke management. Yet the haze redeemed. It concealed war plants. According to the *Telegraph*, "The 'smokeout' is nothing more or less than the application to industry of the smoke-screen used in the past and present in battles at sea."

The worker inflow burdened housing. In January, federal authorities green-lighted home construction and projected nearly one thousand units. Meanwhile, the Harrisburg Chamber of Commerce sought accommodations for arrivals. In April, President Roosevelt sanctioned an "emergency housing program" to "be carried out immediately in the Harrisburg...area." The *Telegraph* asked homeowners to advertise vacancies: "Be Patriotic! Rent Your Spare Room Quickly—Inexpensively." Officials advocated building additions and "doubling up" (house sharing). Miller Brothers and Company forecasted that commuters would move to the city, believing they wanted bus routes' proximity and reduced vehicle use.

Crowds of defense workers on Market Square busing to the Middletown Air Depot. *From the* Evening News. *Courtesy of PennLive.*

Policing the unruly became a priority. Prohibitionists worried about increased alcoholic consumption around military installations. Newspapers reported frequent crimes, in some cases by soldiers. Authorities apprehended a resident threatening President Roosevelt.

Prostitution and social disease menaced Harrisburg. Bawdyhouse raids and harlot arrests multiplied. National, state and municipal agencies crusaded to curb promiscuous sex and venereal infection. The Army Third Corps command supported the American Social Hygiene Association's program to combat syphilis. Colonel James A. Stevens at Indiantown Gap backed Vance C. McCormick's request for cash "to protect the soldiers and war workers" from an "illness as deadly as enemy bullets." In like manner, a state motor police officer explained the prostitute's threat to the military. He endorsed strict law enforcement and closed brothels. Rehabilitative instruction, he believed, should follow quarantining.

Coincidentally, the Rio scheduled *No Greater Sin*. The film portrayed a community's emergence as a manufacturing hub and struggle against social disease. The release received praise and the newspaper headline "A Movie Endorsed." The Catholic Legion of Decency took a different view, citing a standard criticism of "Sex Hygiene" pictures.

Black people suffered employment snubs. The State Council of Defense sympathized but shunned remediation. Dr. Arnaud C. Marts, its executive director, "deplored the discrimination" but warned that "Negroes themselves will make a great mistake if they promote the race issue aggressively at this time."

Black people remained separated and badgered. The Inter-Racial Study Group, meeting at the Forster Street YMCA, examined the "Race Myth." The State's *In This Our Life* dramatized a potential injustice to a Black man, but a columnist plugged, "In Which the Girl Out to Beat Life Yields + Death!" Beyond this reference to a white character, the column made no mention of the race angle nor the Black stars. The *Evening News* advertised the "Sprinklin's Sambo" as "Firestone Victory Values." The Fifth Street Methodist Church's Dramatic Club planned a "Coon Valley Minstrel" show, apparently unaware of the pejorative.

The summons to arms irked and inflamed some people. Sportsmen complained about hunting's prohibition. Letters to Michael Season's column With Rod and Gun: Outdoors favored continuance for diversional and psychological purposes, as well as weapons' education. Season revealed the stoppage of fishing tackle manufacture and suggested anglers carpool because of gas rationing. Italian Lake incited provocation. The word *Italian* deleted from a postcard sparked the *Harrisburg Sunday Courier*'s repartee that the sender failed to recognize the contributions of Italy's natives.

The defense call furthered health. In February, the municipal Council for Physical Fitness linked recreation to "Hale America." Officials contemplated augmenting Reservoir Park's croquet section and permitting evening tennis. In March, the annual Gold Medal Basketball Tournament ran as scheduled. Such activity aided physical fitness and entertained war workers. Promotions pushed milk and bread consumption, warning, "Hitler's secret weapon is our lack of the B-1 vitamin." By March, Washington had submitted guidelines for a proper diet.

Surprisingly, attention soon turned to the postwar. In February, milk retailers talked of the future. The Kiwanis Club heard a Memorial Day speaker argue for a peace negotiated by pragmatists, not idealists.

3

# DUTY AMID CONTROVERSIES AND AFFLICTIONS

## July 1942–December 1942

In 1942, Harrisburg perfected civilian safeguards, enacted federal programs and supported defense drives. Industry boomed. Businesses, schools, organizations and churches provided patriotic services. The war emergency triggered changes and challenges.

The city conducted some successful air raid drills. Blackouts required building lights out. Violators chanced arrests, fines and jailing. Sirens announced tests, and an August exercise caught residents off guard with many in Reservoir Park and on River Island. Another in November startled shoppers and found retailers' lights aglow. A woman suffered heart failure. Daylight tests mandated residents indoors, curbed vehicles and bus passenger drop offs. Churches held congregations until an all clear.

Local authorities received training in toxic gases, bomb handling and incendiary dousing. Fire companies enhanced apparatus, adding four pumpers, hose lengths and gas masks.

The schools adapted. Pupils stayed inside during alerts. Officials advised the fingerprinting of elementary children as a precaution for air attacks and large-scale evacuations that could part them from parents. Gas raids became a studied topic. The district bought war insurance.

On Sixth and Dauphin Streets, the National Theater showed Sunday air raid films for educational purposes.

Harrisburg experienced defiance. Several dismissed the seriousness of the precautions. Housewives hung clothes during drills. Officials quieted all sirens and bells welcoming the New Year to prevent confusion with raid signals.

Stealing increased. Thefts of sand, ration books and a tire ended Saturday evening drills since "thieves took advantage to loot stores."

Defense elicited retailers' self-promotion. The Lucas Paint Store marketed blackout shades "complete with clips and sill bracket." Clothing for college women featured "luminous" garments.

Song, film, radio and cartoons mimicked blackouts. The Rio's *The Yanks Are Coming* introduced "There Will Be No Blackout of Democracy." At the State's *George Washington Slept Here*, Jack Benny asked, "When did you buy this house—during a blackout?" Radio aired a homicide drama during enforced darkness. The *Superman* comic strip illustrated Metropolis's initial drill. The *Harrisburg Sunday Courier*'s serialized defense blunders, picturing a woman chasing an unleashed dog during an alert and being told the animal should be restrained.

Combating incendiaries touched comics. *Moon Mullins* showed Moon placing a water-filled pail atop a house to extinguish firebombs. *Joe Jinks* gave instruction on incendiary control.

The press reported diversionary moments. Two boys took shelter in a trash can at Third and Market. An air warden removed a bewildered turtle ambling Third Street to the safety of the Capitol grounds.

Harrisburg garnered recognition. An editorial applauded residents for compliance. An out-of-town sheet commended the city's program. An Allison Hill air raid station ranked highest in Pennsylvania. Mayor Milliken, taking credit, called his measures the "finest in the East."

Security confronted a semblable threat. To be sure, radio warned of foreign nationals. Enemy aliens made court appearances. Authorities identified military districts shielded from spying and sabotage. A Nineteenth Street simulation had German agents smashing a local air raid station. Additionally, the FBI scheduled a conference on domestic defense.

Officials took the alleged peril seriously. In July, a Middletown Air Depot guard spotted suspected saboteurs, but police failed to locate them. Authorities investigated a carrier pigeon seen at the Market Street Bridge. They forbid picture taking. Furthermore, police banned false-faced Santas out of fear of the enemy.

No evidence surfaced of subversion, but media created a fantasy fare. The funnies evoked a domestic danger. *Pam* noted a sabotage case, *Dan Dunn* mentioned a fifth columnist and *Little Mary Mixup* made a reference to an internal menace. In November, the city library shelved *Sabotage! The Secret War Against America* by Michael Sayers and Albert E. Kahn. Radio aired a wake-up call. Downtown theaters repeatedly ran the theme in *Foreign Agent*,

John Todoroff and Anthony Dimov seek shelter during an air raid drill. *From the* Evening News. *Courtesy of PennLive.*

*The Daring Young Man*, *Underground Agent*, *Little Tokyo*, *U.S.A.* and *Let's Get Tough*. The nation confronted spies in *The FBI Front*, *Mr. Blabbermouth*, *Secret Enemies* and *Secrets of the Underground*.

The War Department recruited Harrisburg's youths. Registrations, call-ups and enlistments swelled. The military prized conscripts with technical skills. In July, the army sought men possessing sailing backgrounds for swimming tanks. Draft boards mustered eighteen- and nineteen-year-old boys and considered calling fathers. Some lost physical disability status and received 1-A reclassification.

Recruiting intensified. The navy and marines visited the city. A Navy Day program at the Capitol inducted enrollees, accompanied by school students marching down streets.

Most men complied, but some evaded. Four claimed essential occupations yet remained 1-A. A few failed to return occupational questionnaires or neglected to communicate address changes. Authorities apprehended a draft opponent in Boston and asked the FBI to locate two others. A clergyman, a Church of the Living God minister presiding over a flock of twelve, spurned the call. Several applied for war objector status. A Church of the Brethren member ended up in a labor encampment. All this happened while a downtown theater showed *For Me and My Gal,* a film echoing World War I draft avoidance.

Bond promotion exemplified Harrisburg's patriotism. Store employees breakfasted on "Coffee MacArthur" and "Doughnuts Doolittle." Requests went to retailers to show the American flag. A "gaily-decorated trailer" roved about, aiding sales.

Rallies headlined celebrities. Bud Abbott and Lou Costello appeared in August. Paulette Goddard and William Gargan substituted for Rita Hayworth in September. Goddard's orchids sold for $5,000 and Gargan's tie for $2,000. Johnny Morris, spokesman for Philip Morris cigarettes, met the mayor.

Harrisburg welcomes Hollywood's Bud Abbott and Lou Costello for a bond drive. *From the* Evening News. *Courtesy of PennLive.*

Exhibitions backed the drive. On July 21, residents observed overhead aircraft, a parachute display and draftee enrollments. A P-39 Aircobra fighter perched on Market Square. In another spot, onlookers invested a dollar or more to signature bombshells. Most inscribed their names. However, some imprecated the Axis: "Nuts to Hitler," "Deliver to Japan" and "Smack the Japs."

Stunts drew attention to the push. Fire Chief Earl Swartz clambered up a fire ladder for purchases, which extended to the fourth story of the new Dauphin County Courthouse. In an act of lofty daredevilry, flagpole dancers Betty and Benny excited a crowd on a small platform above the Square's Dauphin Building.

Movie houses participated. Theaters planned rallies. They offered bond buyers free admission. The State designated any child a "Junior Commando" when admitted to see an uncharged picture.

Businesses contributed. Retailers and industries urged employees to join payroll bond buying. By mid-December, eighty-one firms signed on. Food stores and merchants sold bonds and stamps. Their ads expedited the campaign. The Old Drum Brand, a whiskey company, urged buying to "bowl over the Axis," the Brann and Stuart Company's plug exploited U.S. war prisoners and the Stroehmann Brothers Company declared bonds the 1942 Christmas gift. At the Harrisburg Wearing Apparel Company on North Sixth Street, personnel bought from pay raises.

Slogans enlivened marketing. The Chamber of Commerce persuaded retailers to ply "Buy Share of Freedom." Motion picture theaters heralded "Salute to Our Heroes" month in August and "Avenge Pearl Harbor" for December. A newspaper quipped, "Better to buy bonds today than to have bonds around our neck tomorrow."

Officials conferred awards and recognition. Girls delivered kisses for stamps, an episode aped in *Bringing Up Father*, when the strip's daughter smooched for $5,000 bonds. Kipona's river festivities gave defense investments for boat racing. A future art show promised bond awards. The Equitable Life Insurance Company commended agents. Harrisburg Hospital, Central Iron and Steel and PPL received the Minute Man Flag for payroll purchasing.

Civic groups took part. The Kiwanians welcomed actress Gloria Stuart and singer Barry Wood. The Washington Camp, No. Eight, Patriotic Order Sons of America, bought $1,000 in bonds. The Harrisburg Chapter Sixty-Four, Order of Ahepa, established a $180,000 minimum. City police committed $5,000. The Harrisburg Firemen's Relief Association voted for $20,000. The American Legion Auxiliary, Unit Twenty-Seven, planned stamp sales.

A program acknowledged labor's role. Enya Gonzalez, a Filipina opera singer, performed, and Lieutenant Bartholomew Passanante, a Philippine war veteran, spoke.

Women volunteered services, accepting partial responsibility for Dauphin County's quota. In November, they crusaded for an aircraft with the motto "Buy a Bomber" to be christened *Women of Dauphin County, Pennsylvania*. In December, ladies manned booths at eleven locations.

The press encouraged carriers to sell. In September, the *Patriot* and the *Evening News* announced their paperboys sold over $169,000 in stamps and bonds.

One woman uttered a confession. Her bond purchase came from divorce funds, but she could bear her husband more than Hitler.

Dauphin County aimed to meet war costs, prevent inflation, urge frugality and support postwar rebuilding. *Freckles and His Friends* reinforced what stamps financed in a September cartoon.

Gasoline rationing continued. Teachers in schools issued the standard *A* allowances with requests for greater amounts pleaded to area boards. Petitions soon depleted applications. Some motorcyclists received *D* rations for essential travel. Officials gave Harrisburg's visitors enough fuel to depart. Regulations required drivers to attach allotment stickers on the lower right edge of their back window.

By late July, gas sales dropped. Motorists tanked with newly issued script. Officials warned gas dealers about unattached coupons. They had to be sure that ration books carried the numeral identifications of license plates. Middletown Air Depot employees found their appeals for supplements denied. Rather than asking for more gas, an editorial encouraged motorists to share vehicles.

Rubber rationing limited commodities. By mid-October, officials mandated a five-tire ceiling for cars. Restrictions impacted boots, and six styles underwent controls.

Illegal connivances skyrocketed. Unlawful tire sales and thefts increased. A tire ring operated. Authorities broke up a black market worth $1 million. The gang colluded in five states and conspired locally. Law enforcement named at least two hundred culprits.

Hollywood dramatized the pinch. In August, the Rio billed *Rubber Racketeers*, an exposé revealing tire crooks and "tire bootleggers." Subsequently, the theater ran *White Cargo*, a tale of an African rubber plantation and a reminder of the product's shortage.

Authorities certified bicycles and cars for essential services. Defense workers could purchase bikes. The Harrisburg Taxicab and Baggage Company acquired permits for five cars.

Harrisburgers adjusted to shortages. Rationing bound a pound of sugar for each fourfold pounds of peach preserves. In September, the coffee allotment plunged to 65 percent of the previous ration. By October, drinkers resigned themselves to a daily cup. Officials established a one-pound allowance for five weeks. Criticism fell on hoarders. The Harrisburg Consumers' Committee advocated a meat intake reduced to forty ounces weekly. Women traveled house to house to explain the sacrifice.

Stove rationing became law in December. Appliance restrictions intended to reserve heating equipment for voluntary conversions from oil to coal.

The Office of Price Administration heightened price administration. It listed cost ceilings. Air raid wardens explained postings to merchants. Storeowners conferred at the courthouse, and officials conducted surveys. Checks discovered low compliance, with half of the retailers derelict. The office passed on complaints to a regional OPA in the city's Blackstone Building. Its agents heard grumbling about coffee charges and barroom rum increases. It investigated price raises by PPL and required coffee tradesmen to submit stock-holding records.

In mid-November, wage stabilization offices operated in Harrisburg, emanating from the U.S. Department of Labor's Wage and Hour and Public Contracts Division. Milliken resisted a fair rent official's selection for the division. Judging the appointment ill-advised, he refused to volunteer aid. William E. Good, the federal administrator, overlooked the mayor and set up posts, despite the school board's denial of facilities. Eventually, the division was housed in thirty-two locations and counted forty thousand rental properties in the region.

The victory garden program engaged the city as information about soils and fertilizers became widespread. Compost piles produced humus. The neutralization of vandals and rabbits proved effective. Educational director William J. Ross reported that under the banner "Garden for Defense," more plots came to life than before. Adults and children worked community lands. State employees, defense workers and housewives labored. The garden force reached 1,257. Output satisfied food requirements of 3,826 individuals. The Melrose and Shimmell PTAs gave kids gardening tributes.

The demand for scrap prompted drives. Women turned in food fats and hose. Children rounded up metals. Municipal ash and garbage trucks transferred collections to depositories. Accumulations included artifacts. The city donated displayed cannons. Civil War ball and shell as well as a 1918 war medal piled the heap. Bowman's tendered old war shells.

Camp Curtin Junior High School students collect keys for metal scrap, supervised by Mary Elizabeth Schlayer. *Photograph by Ensminger Studio from the* Harrisburg Telegraph. *Courtesy of PennLive.*

The campaign gathered an assortment. Firefighters retrieved a submerged ferry cable from the Susquehanna. The *Telegraph* offered a dismantled Goss press. Republicans surrendered an old elevator. Donors threw in iron-based toys, lawn mowers, radiators and Japanese-made products. The Evangelical Press furnished metal. Montgomery and Company scrapped a safe. Sears Roebuck assembled old cars and used tires. A heating boiler came from an unknown source.

Clergy did their part. The Diocese of Harrisburg promised to scavenge churches and schools.

Some scrap remained unexploited. The city decided against the extraction of disused streetcar rails on North Sixth because of expense and inadequate asphalt. Officials searched for active artillery shells buried in Wildwood Park after World War I, but their location remained elusive.

Tin wastage and criminal shenanigans hampered the effort. Labeled and unflattened cans among garbage and rubbish lost value. Requests for homeowners to process containers went unheeded. Thieves stole curbside drops, leading one letter to charge "sabotage." Ash and Garbage Collection Bureau employees and junk dealers schemed to finagle scrap. Larceny accusations and bail postings followed.

An editorial lamented a subdued enthusiasm. Residents seemed more generous giving blood. But Pearl Harbor's memory redeemed the city. A

Salvage for Victory Committee's push for 900 tons of metal surged 276 beyond projection. Meanwhile, stores recorded three tons of fats delivered. The hauls avenged December 7. Harrisburgers had taken a "slap at the Jap."

Rewards marked scrap collection. Children dropping off five pounds of metal received free movie admissions. The city and the Red Cross earned money from scrap sales. A Pabst Blue Ribbon ad thought scrapping fostered neighborliness. Dauphin County Salvage for Victory Committee participants qualified for a War Production Board (WPB) banner.

Film and press made known the urgency. *Salvage*, a short subject, played downtown. Newspapers advised conservation, preservation and substitution. The use of less cooking gas and making do with leftovers, tied to food refrigeration, avoided waste. Federal authorities importuned women to can. They wanted homeowners to consider coal conversion. Beans and fish could replace meat. A column entreated housewives to retain fats and tin cans. One sheet greeted readers with "scrap front fast becoming second front."

Comic strips took off. *Cap Stubbs and Tippie* and *Bringing Up Father* illustrated kids gathering scrap. *Dixie Dugan* plugged the grease drive. Walt Disney pictured Donald Duck removing elastic from his youngers' slingshots and unable to enter his house because he donated the door key.

City schools adjusted to wartime. The new term began with renewed war damage insurance, sufficient staff and students unaffected by employment temptations. National health concerns compelled examinations for high school enrollees. Transportation and blackouts hindered football. The district found busing unavailable for fans. It rescheduled junior high night games to daytime to ease bus service at peak hours. In late September, Superintendent Clarence Zorger expressed worry that student labor permits might create a juvenile delinquency problem like England's.

Education attuned to the emergency. Curricula emphasized science and mathematics, and preflight study introduced pilot training. William Penn's student-run paper ceased publication to conserve. Camp Curtin originated a first aid association. Its Junior Red Cross assembled Christmas articles. Curtin likewise established the Aviation and Model Airplane Clubs. It discussed national defense topics during Book Week and held the patriotic assembly Democracy through the Ages. Meanwhile, Edison filled American Junior Red Cross packages and staged a Red Cross program. Its students organized an aviation group. By mid-November, Penn installed a national High School Victory Corps chapter. Air raid and fire crews stood ready at John Harris.

School youth assisted community campaigns. Camp Curtin's Junior Commandos distributed defensive literature and gathered scrap. Webster's

Edison Junior High School girls gather stockings for salvage with teacher Loraine Heagy in charge. *Photograph by Ensminger Studio from the* Harrisburg Telegraph. *Courtesy of PennLive.*

fifth and sixth graders collected tin, rubber and stockings. Edison, public high schools and Catholic High rummaged for hose. Teens from William Penn sold war stamps.

Parent-teacher associations complemented schools. Edison's membership began Red Cross courses on home nursing and nutrition. Forney's association heard the superintendent outline the schools' wartime role. A county speaker explained the groups' civil task. Foose sponsored a conversation about the war's aim. Catholic High's association planned a musical. Its marching band and choir would render the "Marine Hymn," "The Star-Spangled Banner" and "America."

War's gear-up forced concessions. Shortages necessitated merchandise shifts. For example, an electrical goods store turned to home furnishings. Railroad employees reduced the use of free passes. Harrisburg Steel canceled a picnic. Veterans called off Armistice Day ceremonies conflicting with work hours. Concurrently, holidays became laboring days.

Federal authorities appreciated local enterprise. The Reconstruction Finance Corporation (RFC) advanced assistance. Agreements engaged construction. For instance, the army employed Ritter Brothers and H.B. Alexander and Son. The Herre Brothers won assignment for sewage and drainage in Lebanon. On August 3, Harrisburg Steel received a second E

Accidents caused thousands of homefront casualties. *From the* Evening News. *Courtesy of PennLive.*

award. The American Legion Band accompanied remarks and awards with "America," "Stars and Stripes Forever" and "The Star-Spangled Banner."

Labor's role compelled attention. To satisfy demand, industrialists discussed training. The rail line increased personnel at the city's Pennsy station. A late October estimate placed forty-four thousand men in local manufacturing.

Praise showered the worker. United States Supreme Court associate justice Owen Roberts paid tribute to the blue collar at the Forum. Radio aired an acknowledgement of railroaders. Another broadcast adapted Hollywood's *Joe Smith, American*, a tribute to factory labor. Two films recognizing employees played at downtown theaters, the State's *Wings for the Eagle* and the Rio's *Priorities on Parade*.

The editorial "Workers' Casualties" revealed more non-military deaths than Germans slayed during World War I. It implored that "every worker, and every worker's family, and every employer—and then to the public as a whole—to fight the mounting curve of accidents, both within the factory and outside." A macabre caricature, "This Is How I 'Keep 'Em Rolling,'" sketched a skeletal image in laborer's garb inscribed "CARELESSNESS" with a handheld emblem titled "Daily Industrial Accidents in the U.S." Vehicles identified as "funeral" and "ambulance" enhanced the gruesomeness.

The war's growing intensity activated civic groups. Organizations offered social, informational and welfare programs.

USO affiliates sponsored dances, dedicated the Reist riverboat and celebrated Halloween. They observed holidays and promised Sunday concerts. Their activities included recording radio programs for servicemen abroad, placing posters on buses locating social centers and providing aid to travelers. The North Street Catholic branch, one year old in July, showed Sunday movies.

The *Telegraph* listed weekly events. An advice column asked local men to share their women for USO events.

Hollywood portrayed the USO. The Senate's *Private Buckaroo* screened a performance for soldiers about to leave the United States. *The Yanks Are Coming* at the Rio pictured musical entertainment for troops in training.

Veterans supported war causes. The American Legion sponsored a phonograph collection but with disappointing results. The Disabled Veterans of the World War gave a musical victory show. Jewish veterans gathered moneys for a fighter aircraft.

City Ys stepped up services. The YMCA gave free memberships to servicemen, including bathing, sleeping, food and recreation. Over eleven thousand benefited. A social noted the birth dates of enlistees. Y youths, in recognition of the labor shortage, helped farmers harvest. In mid-October, radio presented *The Cause Men Serve*, commemorating the association's ninety-eight years of existence. Narrator Henry Hull, an actor, described its programs during the Civil War, the Spanish-American War, the First World War and the current struggle. The YWCA publicized activities with a "gansete." The segregated Forster Street chapter heard a military chaplain encourage Black backing for victory and "the realization of true democracy at home." The Phyllis Wheatley branch packed supplies for the Red Cross.

Clubs enacted agendas. An Elks fundraiser and dog show financed its canteen. It voted a $350 donation to the Community Chest and War Fund. The Kiwanians hosted a USO affair and a service flag ceremony. They heard speeches about Winston Churchill, rubber's shortfall and Adolf Hitler. The

Knights of Columbus held a dance and a servicemen's "send-off party." The Lions participated in a riverboat sing. They listened to a "rapid-fire address," a cautioning of the war's length and difficulty. Captain A.A. Nichoson, the speaker, tongue-lashed Americans as "too soft" and "asleep."

Sororities were enlightened. Harrisburg's Daughters of the American Revolution lent ears to a diatribe damning appeasement. At the Business and Professional Women's Club, the American Association of University Women took in a reporter's psychiatric insights relating to the war.

The Junior League gave the Red Cross a canteen vehicle. The Dorcas Club, a neighborhood association, purchased yarn for soldiers' pullovers and covers. The Big Sister Club readied presents for servicemen in Great Britain. The Quota Club prepared Christmas stockings for patients at Indiantown Gap's hospital. Along with book donations, the Rotary Club worked a USO service. Members heard a speech about artificial rubber. The Exchange Club helped the USO. It discussed poisonous gas and the postwar times. The Harrisburg Study Club educated itself on wartime nutrition. Before the Civic Club, a speaker argued that only religion could nourish and maintain democracy.

The war engaged business and consumer groups. The Junior Chamber of Commerce listed USO activities and locations. It patronized a dance and WAAC enlistment. The parent Chamber of Commerce was informed about the Coral Sea battle. The Consumer League of Greater Harrisburg convened a canning seminar.

Charitable agencies became more active. The Community Chest and War Fund drive sought more than $125,000 but reported a shortfall. The Red Cross supervised surgical dressing, nurses' aid and nutritional training. It collected magazines for the overseas-bound and facilitated family allowance paperwork. Other services included travel meals, emergency furloughs, cash borrowings and private advice. Care was extended to prisoners by the forwarding of communications and foodstuffs.

The Red Cross replaced the mobile blood unit stationed on Second and Pine Streets. A permanent site availed in the William Elder Baily building on Front and South once Harrisburg emerged as one of the nation's blood centers. It posted tallies of donors. City police, firefighters and lawyers answered the call, as did members of the 104th Cavalry. A mother of fifteen children donated. An editorial headed "Coffee Tip" promoted blood giving and promised two cups for each donation.

Clergy underpinned the patriotic and spiritual actions. Churches ministered flag-waving programs and volunteered services. Banner dedications honored servicemen. The military received blessings, and Jewish soldiers got special observances. At a Park Street church, a soldier's mother unveiled an honor roll. Clerical contributions aided the Red Cross and the USO. Missionaries hailed Latin America and Russia. Moreover, ministers solemnized Pearl Harbor's anniversary, and "An American Prayer" mixed poetry and devotion.

Spokespeople, both secular and sectarian, beckoned to prayer and the Bible. A Capital Park speaker emphasized the necessity of worship "because of the times in which we live," while a sermonizer urged "prayers for victory." The *Telegraph* printed the regular feature A Daily Prayer, which was complimented by a mother for bestowing "so much comfort." In November, city officials cued residents to regard President Roosevelt's summons to pray and attend church. Mayor Milliken declared October 12 the start of Bible Week. An evangelist referenced the scriptures when cursing Japan's Pearl Harbor attack.

Messages uplifted ideological values. A clergyman said liberties needed to be exercised to be worthy. Loew's distributed free copies of the vicar's sermon sanctioning a people's war from Hollywood's *Mrs. Miniver*. The *Saturday Evening Post* damned Hitler's dogma as "an ersatz religion based on Fuehrer worship." Rabbi Magil chastised the enemy. St. Patrick's rector preached the goals of peace.

But decadence threatened wartime society. At the Forum, the Right Reverend Monsignor Fulton J. Sheen relayed the triple calling to "crush totalitarianism," "purge the sensate culture" and "restore Christian moral order." The Olivet Presbyterian Church's rejection of the lottery for raising war moneys kindled concurrence. An editorial condemned the lottery as one of the "very evils which the home folks allow to prevail." It decried the lottery's impact on "decency and wholesomeness." The Most Reverend George L. Leech pontificated that perverse and immoral conduct damaged the country. Entertainment, photography and literature, he charged, befouled one's person and displeased the Almighty.

Mobilization influenced homemaking. Advisories targeted housewives' care of purchases, possessions and waste. Their responsibilities entailed the creation of "health and endurance and good spirits." Their nature inclined them to use idle hours for wartime duties. Yet it was believed that too much drudgery could tire and cause a "cracking point." The suitable rounds remained: home maintenance, prune canning, lunch packing and fat storage. The heroine of Jan Struther's novel *Mrs. Miniver* typified the homefront role of confronting and resolving daily challenges.

Many women contributed outside the domicile. They worked scrap collections and fundraisers and aided the Red Cross and the police. *Pam* showed their endeavors when its character considered nursing and military services.

Many women found employment. Classified ads called for women as gas station attendants, bank employees and truck drivers. The federal government needed stenographers. Once trained, females acquired jobs as mechanics, welders and bus maintenance aides. The Harrisburg Railways Company's leaders thought of hiring women drivers. The Central Iron and Steel Company welcomed a female drafter. Tied to the new trend, the State ran *Take a Letter Darling*, in which a businesswoman employs a male secretary.

Approval greeted women workers. Film and radio applauded their employment. Milliken announced a week of recognition. A Camel's ad pictured a smiling female employee. *Tillie the Toiler* revealed how girls in training dealt with wolves.

Some found the armed forces enticing but not without ridicule. The movie *Parachute Nurse* and a newspaper editorial lent encouragement to WAAC enrollment. The Women Accepted for Volunteer Emergency Service (WAVES), which offered positions for the U.S. Naval Reserve, recruited women. *Betty Khaki*, a comic strip, jested that female volunteers worried more about men than service. A pun questioned, "Can a woman be happy in the Army? Every other woman has a hat just like hers."

Columnists demanded undiminished appearance despite unconventional roles and hard work, stating that beauty and femininity must be retained. Patricia Lindsey gave cosmetic tips for wartime travel, treatment pointers for excessive facial hair and ideas for walks and climbs to aid the figure. "Do a man's job but remain feminine," she pleaded. Antoinette Donnelly conceded the "doubletime" lifestyle yet argued that image need not suffer. She stated that ladylike attire helped morale and unseemly workplace behavior deserved censure. Cracking chewing gum, going without deodorant and untidy sights offended. She told women to wear perfume and keep legs hair-free. She added, "There is no reason to go overboard for this uniform stuff."

Employed women required new safety precautions and protocol. Goggles protected eyes, hair nets cleared faces and caps protected heads. Mothers wanted day care. City council proposed nurseries, but a monetary shortage blocked the project, and a budget failed appropriation. A childcare facility had been planned for December. The comic strip *Dixie Dugan* discussed its heroine establishing a child center and inquired, "What's Dixie going to do about the baby blitz?" A quip claimed that Russia battles skillfully and furnishes day care readily.

Attractive work and uniform cuts prevailed. Distinct shoes materialized. Accurately sized footwear prolonged stocking life, according to Winifred Raushenbush's publication *How to Dress in Wartime*. Going without and change sparked comments. A wit joked that one rarely overheard "'There's a run in your stocking…' (who has stockings?)" An onlooker deplored the donning of slacks, slighting them as uninflated bloomers.

Bowman's invited Laura Lasley, Lux Laboratories representative, to speak on lingerie preservation. Mixing patriotism with practicality, she warned against negligent cleansing of underthings and advised a tepid Lux lather pressed softly throughout. She imparted girdle advice. Stretch protection required their shielding from hot water, radiators and sunlight.

Newspapers recommended regular contact with the deployed. To upgrade morale, wives and girlfriends wrote about home and neighborhood with humor. Be uncomplaining if the soldier neglects to respond, cautioned Doris Blake. Exhibiting genuine cheer and performing war tasks would be appreciated, she added, and refrain from corresponding about a competing love interest. The editorial "For Letter Writers" listed the USO's suggestions: avoid the war, entertainment, household distresses, political conflicts, neighborhood discord and rumor repetition. Instead, write about family developments and accomplishments. It said mail newspaper articles concerning persons of interest and be upbeat, brief and dependable. A cartoon, *The Mailman Passed Him By*, underscored the letter's "morale-boosting tonic."

In *Guadalcanal Diary*, Richard Tregaskis described marine animation once home tidings arrived: "This afternoon trucks came to dump a pile of gray canvas sacks at Col. Hunt's C.P. It was mail—the first to reach the troops since we landed on Guadalcanal! Each man seemed as happy as if you had given him a hundred-dollar bill at the mere thought of getting mail. And that evening was an orgy of reading. Most of the men had three or four letters each; they sat in circles and read them several times, and read pieces of them to each other."

In-laws could cause conflict. At first, Blake approved of a soldier situating his newlywed inside the family home. She changed her mind, though, believing two women in a household could brew discontent; therefore, "go in for separation roofs, no matter what economies must be practiced." Blake wanted parents to allow a daughter to be at her husband's military station. Also, women had to understand their men's changed demeanor that was brought on by a grisly undertaking.

A plea to write to your soldier. Don't let him down. *From the* Evening News. *Courtesy of PennLive.*

The community comforted transient members of the military. Residents solicited home furnishings and sporting gear for their quarters. Dauphin County issued free marriage licenses. A troupe arranged entertainment with local talent. The Harrisburg Symphony Orchestra granted free admission to a program. A columnist thought a morale booster would be a Thanksgiving invitation to share turkey, an idea reflected in *Dixie Dugan*. For Christmas, the Beta Tau Chapter of the Beta Sigma Phi gave gifts to WAACs.

Those out of sight remained in mind. The Patriot-News Company printed a local news review for staff on military assignment. Patricia Lindsay's column suggested shaving tools as a gift. On Second Street, Ensminger Studios marketed a girl's photograph as the ideal favor.

The war touched children's lives. Their health preoccupied the nation, and a sermon at the Grace Methodist Church raised questions about the conflict's impact.

A couple receives a free marriage license from county clerk C. Wesley Fisher. Walter M. Mumma (*inset*) paid for licenses of all enlisted men applying. *From the* Evening News. *Courtesy of PennLive.*

Children devoted energy to wartime programs. They participated in neighborhood activities such as a flag presentation on the Boas Street School play area and a USO fundraiser at the Royal Terrace Playground. Boy Scouts gathered scrap. They engaged in aviation and defense studies. The Beth El Temple Brownie Troop sponsored a Victory Party, charging a stamp purchase for admission. At the YWCA, Girl Scouts huddled about war work. They surpassed a stamp sale's quota.

Children's behavior came under scrutiny. The editorial "Wartime Halloween" requested love of country by disavowal of mischief. Kids had been stealing scrap receptables. Ministers proposed a curfew requiring youth under sixteen off the streets by 10:30 p.m. Before Christmas, it was approved by the city council.

Wartime culture mirrored children. A poster pressing bond purchases pictured a farmer and two youngsters in a wheat field. Radio detailed their role and applauded the Girl Scouts. Comic strips framed their activities. *Little Mary Mixup* portrayed a hot dog service, *Bringing Up Father* showed kid scrap collectors and *Little Annie Rooney* and *Dixie Dugan* sketched stamp buying. Hollywood's *The Major and the Minor* and *Junior Army* featured military academies. *The Pied Piper* dramatized an elder trekking children across war-torn France. *Scholastic Magazine* rated it the "outstanding film for September."

By mid-1942, Harrisburg's war mentality resounded. Travel curbs raised questions about Romper Day. In spite of transportation difficulties, residents attended a Fourth of July celebration in Reservoir Park, which included a military exercise by the 104th Cavalry.

Harrisburg appreciated the bearing up of America's oldest ally, France. A Free French branch was located in the community. Its flag flew above city hall. In September, the Rio ran *Jungle Siren*, depicting Free French forces in Africa. Continental France's underground movement won praise on radio and in *Joe Palooka*.

The city agonized over China. The *Evening News* publicized a Presbyterian missionary's letter attesting to China's plight. The Community Fund and War Chest requested funds to meet the country's needs. An editorial bade the Chinese good fortune. A missionary spoke of enduring sixty air raids. A Chinese officer addressed a local club. The Rio billed *Bombs Over Burma*, featuring "China's gift to the American screen, Anna May Wong." The show was set along the Burma Road, and the local reviewer lauded the "saga of a fearless Chinese school teacher…braving Jap bullets and planes."

Food propagandized the conflict. Mrs. Gayner Maddox's column remarked, "Chinese shrimp is tribute to our valiant allies."

Japan conquered the Philippines, but the islands mounted a resistance. Radio transmitted President Quezon's description of his people's fight. A program aired the observation of Philippine Commonwealth Day. The Rio ran *Manila Calling*, paying commendation to the Filipino fighters. Loew's showed Americans and natives battling the Japanese in *Somewhere I'll Find You*.

Axis stereotypes issued from the press and cinema. The Italians emerged least sinister in these portrayals. Puns conceded little respect. Hollywood poked fun at Italy's ineptitude and cartooned the country as a burdensome Germany ally. *Cairo* showed "hysterical" sons of Italy startled by gunfire and pleading to give up. *Joan of Ozark* derided an Italian spy as "foolish." *The Boogie Man Will Get You* mocked a flyer with the derisive "Baciagalupi" as "mad."

The city saw a menace in the German. Funnies caricatured monocled autocrats, both haughty and arrogant. *The Pied Piper* demonstrated their inhumanity, picturing Nazi planes strafing fleeing civilians. Another Nazi toady, a Romanian, appeared in the Rio's *A Date with the Falcon*.

The most contempt branded Japanese. Portraits demonized their character, conduct and physiognomy. They were set apart and were portrayed as treacherous, cowardly, uncivilized and immoral. John Henrik Marsman's publication *I Escaped from Hong Kong* spoke on this, stating that the Japanese starved Americans and mistreated prisoners. *Yankee Doodle* portrayed them firing on a downed pilot, as did the movie *Wake Island*. *Captain Yank*, another strip, had them using poison. A Harrisburger complained of abuse while in their hands.

These accusations culminated in decades of racism and slurs ranted from the screen and press. Harrisburgers viewed reels of disparagement in *They All Kissed the Bride*, *Private Buckaroo*, *Foreign Agent*, *Wake Island*, *Manila Calling* and *Busses Roar*. *Captain Yank* reinforced motion pictures with a "yellow murderers" degradation.

The racialization of Japan dehumanized its people, and subhuman renditions proliferated. Hollywood lessened Japanese people to *Invisible Agent*'s snake and *Manila Calling*'s monkeys. The *Evening News* likened them to insects, a beast and chimpanzees. A pun implied a two-headed creature. *Dan Dunn* and *Draftie* called them rats.

Officials assured Harrisburgers that Kipona, an annual celebration, originated from a non-Japanese source. Editorials became nastier during the December 7 anniversary. The *Telegraph* charged the "Pearl Harbor killing of women and children" uncovered the "military cowardice" of the "flying yellow Japs." The *Evening News* indicted the Japanese for "treachery," name-calling them "unmoral…savages" and demeaning the "little brown men" who "stab us in the back."

The public seemed fascinated by aviation. Gallup polls indicated a belief in winning by air and a desire for air corps precedence. Alexander de Seversky's *Victory through Air Power* and radio appearance vouched the thesis. In a volume carried by Harrisburg's library, Al Williams's *Air Power* "sketches and outlines the structure and visionary plans for a type of warfare which was regarded as a futuristic mechanical dream, until it burst upon Europe."

Press and public took up the craze. The *Telegraph* supplicated for flyers and serialized Bomber Briefs. One excerpt advocated banning beans since air studies demonstrated their gastrointestinal unsettlement when winged. Short fiction told of pilot training and of the autogiro's value. Whitcomb's store on South Cameron Street sold model plane kits, and 3,500 people attended an open house at the Farm Show Building's aviation school.

Bombers accrued special acclaim. *Scorchy Smith* hailed the Boeing B-25 as the "best medium bomber in the business." But no bomber equaled the applause for the B-17. Newspapers recorded their missions and, in one case, a crew's safe return. Headlined the "New Kings of Bombers," B-17 replicas marketed bonds and decorated an actress's veil. The Colonial booked the British-made *Flying Fortress*, revealing that "the real stars of the picture are the Flying Fortresses themselves."

The *V* and Victory symbols permeated Harrisburg. The *V* earmarked foods, air drills, nursing trainees and Community and War Chest efforts. The *Telegraph* cited three *V*s: "Vitamins, vegetables, and victory." Its Roundabout columnist linked the *V* to Christmas ornaments. Onlookers at the recreation boat's Independence Day ceremony noticed a bird flyover in a *V*. *Iceland* entertained State audiences with skaters in a *V* alignment. One wit suggested a "*V* for Victory" lapel piece made from a chicken wishbone for morale. The word *Victory* marked Knights of Columbus parties, a Catholic USO Club terrace, a horse in *Dixie Dugan*, a new ready-to-wear store, a balanced diet, a radio program, a soup and a minister's sermon. Loew's ran *Pete Smith*'s *Victory Vittles* short.

Other markers inculcated patriotism. The eagle embellished crochet patterns, carrying dynamite sticks in a call for unity. The bird adorned a Hoover's ad, asserting, "Keep up the homes we're fighting for." Stars formed a pie. They ringed the background of a Community and War Chest promotion. As freedom's ideal, radio programed the Statue of Liberty. The monument appeared in Alfred Hitchcock's *Saboteur* when an enemy agent plunges to his death from its upheld arm.

Publications available to Harrisburgers fictionalized the conflict. Helen MacInnes portrayed anti-Nazi themes in *Above Suspicion* and *Assignment in Brittany*. Martha Albrand's *No Surrender* praised "the dauntless Dutch underground." A Spanish Civil War veteran's agony at the hands of foreign agents intrigued readers of Dorothy B. Hughes's *The Fallen Sparrow*. *The Seventh Cross* by Anna Seghers, which segmented in the *Telegraph*, made known a German resistance to Hitler.

Downtown movie houses booked more war. The Rio's *Atlantic Convoy* and the Senate's *The Navy Comes Through* dramatized anti-submarine actions. Bomber crews escaped Nazi clutches in the British-made *One of Our Aircraft Is Missing* at the Loew's and *Desperate Journey* at the State. A New York reporter fled Germany in the Rio's *Berlin Correspondent*. *Stand by for Action* at the Loew's screened naval engagement against the Japanese, saluted as "the best of the recent Navy pictures bar none." The Colonial's *Wake Island* heroized the last stand of Marines at an island bastion, praised as "the best of our war pictures and will do a great deal to bolster the national policy."

Hollywood rendered the domestic scene. In *Enemy Agents Meet Ellery Queen*, Detective Queen befuddles spies. *The War Against Mrs. Hadley* portrayed an isolationist's conversion to intervention. Patriotic flag-waving pervaded *Yankee Doodle Dandy*, and military exercises highlighted *Seven Days Leave*. *A Man's World* told of a bawdyhouse in a foreign country, a stain reminiscent of the city. In December, *The Palm Beach Story* provided escape.

Documentaries and shorts edified. The Rio billed *United We Stand*, a historical narrative covering the twenty years between the world wars. The War Activities Committee of the Motion Picture Industry promised *Salvage*, *Manpower Mobilization*, *Paratroops*, *Transportation* and a Disney production about fats and greases. At the Senate, *A Letter from Bataan* urged homefront support. *Middletown Goes to War*, a film of the Tuberculosis and Health Society of Harrisburg and Dauphin County, described the conflict's impact on health as consequences of population growth, industrial tensions and social strains.

Movies became a passion. Their appeal developed "a wartime pastime that an audience of roughly 90 million per week attended avidly."

Americans listened to four hours of radio daily. Local stations aired the war. WHP's *Littletown*, a dramatic series, traced the conflict's impact on the average person. WKBO's *America's Town Meeting* concerned defense workers and housing problems. WJZ recognized the nation's railroads and broadcasted actress Madeleine Carroll's warning of great loss due to accidents in the factory and at home. WHP unmasked enemy propaganda, offered a series titled *Commandos* and scheduled Maxwell Anderson's *The Eve of St. Mark*, a play about an American soldier missing in the Philippines.

Stores merchandised war toys. Wood and cardboard replaced metal military games. Joe the Motorist Friend advertised tanks, model airplanes, soldiers' outfits and a naval fleet. Gibbs Peoples Service Stories carried a tank, a jeep, a military truck and an aircraft with a shelter. Bushey Whitcomb's selections included a submarine and army train. By mid-December, retailers reported heavy sales.

Harrisburgers saw dogs doing their bit. Walt Disney's Donald Duck tugged Bolivar, his St. Bernhard, toward a recruiting station. The Rio's *Blondie for Victory* enrolled Daisy and her pups to raise funds. The Loew's *Eyes in the Night* starred the seeing eye Friday aiding a blind investigator to solve a murder implicating spies. The Rio billed *War Dogs*, screening a police dog's drilling for wartime duty, a euphemism for German shepherds.

Music relieved worry. Conductor Ruby Zwerling thought performances quieted jitters and remedied "wartorn [*sic*] nerve and mental anguish." The Harrisburg Symphony Orchestra's new season hailed, "Music is necessary in wartime even more so than in days of peace." On Saturday evenings, CBS's *Lucky Strike Hit Parade* presented the country's favorite numbers.

Tunes intimated loss. "Don't Sit under the Apple Tree" and "Just as Though You Were Here" evoked loneliness. "White Christmas" and "I'm Waiting for Ships That Never Come" envisioned longing. A recruit's song pined "Ma, I Miss Your Apple Pie," and a parent's absence admonished "Be a Good Soldier While Your Daddy's Away." "Last Call for Love" and "We Shall Meet Again" suggested parting and goodbyes. Encouraging correspondence composed "Just a Letter from Home," as thoughts and waiting did for "A Boy in Khaki—A Girl in Lace." Radio and film introduced ditties that Market Square's J.H. Troup Music House sold on disc.

Music aroused bellicosity and flag waving. "We've Just Begun to Fight," "I Like a Military Tune" and "Praise the Lord and Pass the Ammunition" summoned with the latter, leaving no doubt what side God chose. "Anchors Aweigh," "Semper Fidelis" and the "Marine Hymn" honored services. "There'll Always Be an England" recognized an ally. "Der Fuehrer's Face" bashed the Axis countries. Catchphrases and images such as "Song of Freedom" and "There Will Be No Blackout of Democracy" inspired, whereas "Song of America" invoked love of country. "When the Lights Go on Again" presaged peace, and "Six Jerks in a Jeep" humorized military life.

Lyrics pictured homefront realities. "People Like You and Me," "Let's Bring New Glory to Old Glory" and "We've Got a Job to Do" called for unity. "On the Swing Shift" and "Payday" tuned defense work and worker loyalty. "Cooperate with Your Air Raid Warden" and "Zip Your Lip" ordered civilians to sacrifice. "That's Sabotage" implied a wobbly romance. "I'm Wacky for Khaki" evinced female infatuation. The risqué confessed "You Can't Say No to a Soldier," "I Said Yes" and "He Loved Me till the All Clear Came."

Controversy brewed over Sabbath cinema. The *Telegraph* announced sardonically the practice of the Catholic USO center on North: "Sure they have Sunday movies and so far lightning hasn't hit the building." The USO Council met to consider the question. In December, a report contrasted Harrisburg's recreation with Richmond, Virginia. The Virginia city permitted Sunday films.

A tire and gas saving "skip stop" at Locust and Second Streets. *From the* Evening News. *Courtesy of PennLive.*

Another issue stemmed from river bridges. Toll-collecting backed up military traffic. The Keystone Automobile Club and the *Telegraph* wanted the state to liberate the Market and Walnut Street crossings.

Heavy traffic burdened city streets. A staggered-hours remedy opened stores at 10:00 a.m. and closed them eight hours later. Some merchants opened earlier, but industries promised to comply. Officials rewarded cooperative retailers.

The Harrisburg Railways eliminated halts and routes to relieve congestion. It publicized the locations of "skip stops." Some Herr Street and Hill residents complained. The Pennsylvania Station established a bus park, but congestion and overloads remained. The company added more vehicles to its fleet and asked women to shop early. Rationing rides came under consideration. Bus drivers grumbled about motorists occupying their spaces. Nevertheless, the ODT liked the staggered hours.

Labor needs reached thirty-seven thousand by July. Defense industries and government construction suffered. Insufficient hands for garage mechanics and ash collectors persisted. The United States Employment Service (USES) appraised the community's workforce. The *Evening News* told readers that the war concerned females as well as men.

Employers scrambled. While the Harrisburg Dairies reported an expected employee shortage, the Gibson Roofing Company sought roofers. The symphony orchestra replaced those on military call. The Harrisburg Community Theater assigned two parts to an actor. Schools announced sufficient staff, while county prisoners harvested crops. Requests to the employed to transfer to war-related work resulted in three hundred shifts by late October. Many worked jobs without training and experience. Classified ads reflected a skilled labor deficiency.

In the twenty-four months before December 1942, Harrisburg and Dauphin County populations increased by five thousand. Arrivals received welcomes boasting of the municipality's benefits. Doutrich's store greeted newcomers, and Miller's promised to satisfy their shopping.

Relief roles dropped off. The Chamber of Commerce established a Manpower Advisory Committee. It exhorted unemployed men and women to find work.

Housing stayed inadequate. The scarcity impacted low-income groups and contributed to juvenile delinquency.

Utility service and heating fuel were squeezed. Habitual and unnecessary telephone calls instigated an effort to eradicate "telephonitis…America's most common disease." Arnold Coal and Supply Company implored homeowners to cut consumption. A newspaper argued for conversion to coal.

Soldiers found refuge in Harrisburg. Outside the city were military installations at Indiantown Gap, New Cumberland, Mechanicsburg, Middletown and Carlisle. Railroads carried soldiers in and out throughout the day.

Streetwalkers plied their trade. Ten brothels operated on North Sixth and Seventh Streets, and police raided them. They nabbed prostitutes on Cowden, Mulberry, Grace and Verbeke and in the Seventh Ward.

Venereal disease broke out. Authorities sought measures, and a health institute met. The Federal Security Board, the Third Service Command and the commonwealth studied the problem. Federal health departments became involved. The FBI convened in the city. The state police commissioner favored quarantining prostitutes. He advocated concerted action across jurisdictions. He feared Axis agents mingling with ladies of the night.

February 3 was Social Hygiene Day. The country's communities assembled to stress the fight against veneral disease.

Patrolman Charles Ross (the author's father) points to where Mable A. Harris's body was found raped and murdered by a soldier. *Photograph by Ensminger Studio from the* Harrisburg Telegraph. *Courtesy of PennLive.*

Newspapers chronicled misbehavior by uniformed men. Drinking, intoxication, brawls, beatings, stabbings, rapes and murder shattered the city's calm. A girl accused a soldier of enticement and confinement. An enlisted man attempted suicide. The *Telegraph* told of a drunken lieutenant colonel stumbling about and counseled soldiers that the uniform did not condone such behavior. The Earl E. Aurand Post of the Veterans of Foreign Wars, acting as an auxiliary, helped police cope with drunkenness.

Sentiment grew to restrict alcohol. The *Telegraph* supported drinking establishments' voluntary prohibition for soldiers "as a practical, commonsense solution of a problem that has been developing in the community for some time." Some thought a similar curfew should apply to defense workers. Besides, sale halts could curb prostitution since many propositions occurred in taprooms.

Police Chief Blough believed a dry area around army bases would be helpful. The *Evening News* recalled World War I's victory without alcohol and demonized booze, adding, "The war will end all the more quickly with victory if liquor is defeated first."

Mischief sullied the city. In Third Corps area states, Pennsylvania led with vice. A November statement placed the city behind one other for increased incidents of venereal infection inside the commonwealth. Warnings went out to residents about the ill effects of slot machines. One correspondence to the *Evening News* downplayed the Axis by foretelling its defeat once enemies internal—drink and gambling—faded. Norman Marsh's *Dan Dunn* addressed the exploitation of soldiers and workers by numbers' racketeers. On another tack, a Harrisburger discouraged offensive language and excessive cursing.

Youngsters misbehaved. Parental supervision dropped off as mothers worked and fathers enlisted. Youth crime rose. In July, fifteen-year-old girls attempted to solicit servicemen. Officers detained them once they received blood and health tests. In November, a girl tossed a pebble at a barroom window. The next month, two fourteen-year-old females received physicals following fraternization.

Delinquencies alarmed elders. Ministers and the *Evening News* favored a curfew. The Dauphin County Council of Christian Education organized a committee. Weekly religious instruction gained currency. Before Christmas, clergy gathered with Milliken to address the situation.

Newspapers continued to describe crimes committed by Black people as "Negro" without ascribing a racial identification to crimes committed by white people. Allegations included theft, robbery, larceny, assault, stabbings, shootings, prostitution and "truck joyriding." Police broke up a demonstration by Black youths in November, menacing a bar owner and his customers. Reportedly, boys carried pocketknives.

Racial violence disturbed the country. Outbreaks took place at Flagstaff and Phoenix, Arizona, as well as Vallejo, California. A mob lynched a Black man suspected of raping a white female. An editorial in the *Evening News* praising Supreme Court justice James Byrnes's advocacy of "equal justice under the law" said nothing about the murder. In October, Mississippi recorded three mob murders of Black people in a week, one of whom allegedly violated a thirteen-year-old girl.

Excepting schools and brothels, Black and white people lived separately. Redlining, the procedure of public offices snubbing services to selected communities, mapped areas unfit for home financing and business borrowing. Starting at Forster and running to Maclay, Sixth Street exemplified the practice. The Federal Housing Authority exercised an "explicitly racist" disinvestment. The "segregation limited mobility and residential choices for people of color."

Both races went their own ways. White people felt unwelcome in Black neighborhoods and frowned on Black people strolling their streets.

White-owned stores disapproved of Black people trying on clothing. A Black person visiting Harrisburg would be barred from hotel bookings. The municipality barred them from Island Park beach. Comic strips persisted with negative stereotypes, relegating them to unskilled servile roles.

Within their orbits, Black people contributed. A segregated Negro Division of the Dauphin County Republican Party's defense unit formed. Phyllis Wheatley pursued programs. Forster Street harbored a Black USO, later extended to accommodations in the Penn Building on Seventh and Cumberland. In November, Black churches celebrated African Americans posted at Indiantown Gap.

Labor demands liberalized hiring. Classified ads that had excluded Black people changed to calls for white and Black people. In November, the Pennsylvania Railroad, while employing only white males as freight brakemen, employed Black women for light work. Many Black women found prostitution more lucrative.

Some undertakings would have to wait. Vance C. McCormick's Regional Planning Commission requested infrastructural funds but encountered rebuff. The plight of European Jews compelled action. The *Telegraph* believed a Jewish state in Palestine "merits…practical consideration." Charles M. Feller chaired a local effort on behalf of the Jewish National Fund. The Beth El Temple discussed President Roosevelt's promise to bring the Axis to justice.

Newspapers did their wartime bit. With radio weather reports curbed, the press could only print shorted forecasts. Local sheets provided theater maps of military campaigns.

Unfortunately, one Harrisburg paper became a casualty. The *Harrisburg Sunday Courier* published a last issue on September 27, blaming the conflict for its shutdown.

4

# MEETING THE SUMMONS

## January 1943–June 1943

In 1943, the conflict reverted to America's strategic advantage. Pacific and North African victories seized the initiative. Meanwhile, Harrisburg pursued duty's call. Officials consummated civil precautions, engaged national agendas and addressed consequent troubles. Institutions and clubs rallied. A wartime atmosphere pervaded the community.

The city upgraded its alert system. Regulations allowed riders to stay in buses during bad weather but not during an actual attack. Retailers had to install light locks and guarded for thefts. Air raid wardens requested additional sirens so that a drill could be heard to the municipal limits. At the first test sound, streetlights went off. Emergency vehicles replaced an E sticker with an identity pennant. An audible all-clear superseded confusing color-coded signals.

Violations resulted in prosecutions. Abe Cohen paid a penalty for burning a barroom light. One woman claimed an inability to hear an alarm because of deafness but still faced charges. None escaped the enforcement. Soldiers had to obey blackout stipulations.

Mishaps happened, and one was tragic. Injuries stemmed from a fall and a car crash. The excitement killed one person.

Fearing vulnerability, Harrisburg increased defensive measures. The fire company acquired extra pumpers. The police ordered gas masks and whiten helmets. Ten-man "rescue squads" organized to free victims from bombed structures. Training prepared civilians for residents' protection, fire watching, gas mask use, poison gas neutralization and aircraft

*Above*: Looking north up Second Street, an empty Market Square during an air raid alert. *From the* Evening News. *Courtesy of PennLive.*

*Left*: Be careful what you say. *From the* Evening News. *Courtesy of PennLive.*

identification. The local defense council staged simulated air attacks. Plans began to deploy more domestic security. The ODT mapped the city's evacuation.

Harrisburg needed help. The aircraft detection station and the ration board asked for volunteers. Calls went out for six hundred fire watchers. Golfer Bobby Jones, speaking in the city, solicited for voluntary aid, pinpointing air raid surveillance.

In spite of alarms, an editorial questioned the likelihood of Luftwaffe assaults, given Allied progress, yet admitted their feasibility. Insurance firms saw a market. Miller Brothers and Company claimed many war policy sales and reported a continuing demand. Under the banner "EXPECTING A VISITOR?" J.K. Kipp and Son downplayed the prospect of an air strike but advertised war insurance anyway.

Federal authorities safeguarded internal security. The FBI sponsored two clinics to discuss subversion and rumor. The agency reminded residents how loose talk aided espionage.

Harrisburg experienced a bomb scare. What officials thought was an explosive in a parcel at a doorway materialized as a "hamper."

The city prepared for victory gardens in February. The Agricultural Extension Office furnished a planning pamphlet. Mayor Milliken appointed a woman to lead the county committee. Newspapers supplied applications for public land allotments.

Officials pointed up self-cultivation's benefits. With food and transport diverted, residents learned individual responsibility. Besides, gardening promised dietary balance and healthy regimen as well as supplemental provisions. Without needing to purchase many groceries, the family budget could finance bonds and taxes.

Advisories covered gardening's aspects. Best sites, ideal sizes and preferable seeds gained attention. Recommended tool kits suggested beginning with a spade. Sowing tips included soil readiness, seeding alignment, layouts and succession planting. What to avoid took into account "smothered" seedings, lawn destruction, seed potato cultivation, frost warning ignorance and superfluous plants. Crop selections ranged from vegetables to herbs.

For identification, two planks, one three inches wide and the other eighteen, formed a *V*, which leaned on the forefront of a stay plank. Painted strips of six inches in red, white and blue colored the figure.

Mayor Milliken campaigned against despoilers. Ample insecticide stood ready. Authorities apprehended kids romping in a plot, and residents accused boys of removing plants. Warnings notified pet owners to restrain their

Tillers team with Uncle Sam. "The Harrisburg Garden Club suggests you plant a Victory/Vitamin Garden." *From the* Evening News. *Courtesy of PennLive.*

charges. The Harrisburg Humane Society mounted a dragnet to corral wandering canines.

Bunnies were bugbears. Officials promised trapped rabbits would be exiled. Many found themselves on a Susquehanna River island, providing hunters game. The *Evening News* explained methods to frighten and parry, which included spraying lime and dried blood, ringing wetted aromatic lines and encircling snow-white bunding. Cultivating soybeans would "decoy" the critters from surrounding plants.

One woman snared a rat. She tried to kill it by watering down with a hose.

By April, 618 plot licenses had been granted. No unoccupied ground existed. Rains, too heavy or too few, hampered labor. One woman wanted the fire department to water her plot.

The victory gardens succeeded. The mayor won recognition for his yard's crop. Inspection of the Uptown located a mere five lots unworked. The *Telegraph* headlined, "Victory Gardens of Area Produce Large Crops."

The emergency strained resources. A "5 per cent victory tax" from city employees became necessary. With asphaltic mortar unavailable, the highway department repaired streets with a wet gas pitch. Trash collection needed vehicles and drivers. Requests went unanswered when Milliken asked for heating fuel.

Few applied for jobs. Playground directors, lifeguards and common laborers went wanting. Officials considered hiring women for beach duty. Regardless, one resident called for an early opening of swimming facilities. The city limited tennis court availability, since work schedules inhibited their use. One irate citizen complained, claiming grown-ups required diversion.

The bridge fare controversy intensified. Tolls to cross the Susquehanna stoked demands for repeal. The state legislature proposed to liberate the spans over twenty-four months, with moneys extracted from motorist revenues.

The *Telegraph*, aligned with the Keystone Automobile Club of Harrisburg, insisted the bridges be freed. Their levies exploited the driving public of millions to the stockholding and financial advantage, the paper alleged. When in one year 14,131,264 vehicles stopped to pay tolls, the halts bottlenecked traffic.

Residents believed the bridges had been paid for, and West Shore commuters bristled. With military installation across the river, defense laborers fumed. Coal companies resented added delivery expenses. Untolled spans would reduce busing expenses to the West Shore and release bridge employees for church. In fact, the *Telegraph* claimed that tolls jeopardized devotional attendance and commercialized Sunday. The sheet announced, "The horse and buggy days are over!"

Sunday movies heated debate. In a 1940 referendum, Harrisburg banned any future vote for five years. Pennsylvania's supreme court approved, and only the state legislature, not local government, could revise the movie ban.

Idle soldiers moping about changed everything. A proposal legalizing Sabbath cinema provided for theaters to screen no earlier than 2:00 p.m. exclusively to uniformed personnel, including their escorts. In March, a version billed open movie houses inside a fifteen-mile distance from military camps.

Advocates lobbied. The Junior Chamber of Commerce (JCC) cataloged servicemen's remarks, such as "no place to go," "can't go to church all day" and soldiers "don't stop fighting" on Sunday. The chamber contended that the men found Harrisburg allowed escape from training. The *Central Pennsylvania Labor News* wanted workingmen included because films geared a psychological boost. Without Sunday movies, venereal disease would fester as soldiers sought unhealthy play. A letter implied their showing would "protect mothers with daughters of the thrill-seeking age." The *Telegraph* endorsed Sabbath films, as did the JCC and the Republican women's club. Some clergy filed support. Reports had Great Britain and Australia showing Sunday movies, as did some other states.

Nevertheless, dissenters held firm. Ministers opened churches for servicemen, suggested their satisfaction and favored enforcement of the

Blue Laws. One letter feared the relaxation from Sabbath prayer hazarded sensation-driven maidens: "Look at the pitfalls today for young girls."

City officials actually previewed coming attractions on Sundays. The *Telegraph* wondered why soldiers missed a similar privilege. As if to mock the ban, the paper's film column bragged about dispensing one hundred free tickets for a sneak performance of *Bataan*, apparently on a Sunday.

Harrisburg suffered a crime wave. Culprits assaulted, robbed, burglarized, brawled, stabbed and prostituted. Servicemen assailed, thieved, altercated, fornicated and whored. One murdered a city woman. In January, police dispersed a ruckus at the Palestra. Later, soldiers fought on Market Square. County judges warned that ordinances would be executed. The army deployed a police unit.

Vice, prostitution and disease plagued the city. Authorities confiscated slot machines in a pool hall and at two pharmacies. They made arrests in a suspected gambling den. Raids nabbed women in bawdyhouses on Boas, Kunkel, Fulton and North Fifth Streets. Patrolmen seized couples attempting hotel registration and searched parks for fornicators. Milliken denied the existence of criminal syndicates but reported the high numbers of prostitutes arrested, revealed the count of diseased women and maintained the spread of infection came from teens pursuing servicemen. "These kids with mistaken patriotism outnumber the streetwalkers 10 to 1," he declared.

The FBI cautioned that vice debilitated the country's hygiene and spirit, a "softening of our own population" by "street-walking women." It recorded an "Alarming Rise in Sex Crimes." Harrisburg counted 80 percent of the women caught in parks were afflicted with diseases.

The rise of juvenile delinquency became an enigma. A study indicated a 50 percent increase among males and a 100 percent jump among females. Observers blamed broken homes and church absenteeism. Proposed solutions involved school programs, religious participation and parental direction.

The Anti-Saloon League condemned drink for the city's stigmas and proposed 12:00 a.m. curfews at watering places. It pressed federal authorities to regulate military posts. A letter to the *Evening News* disputed rationing healthful commodities while manufacturing and retailing liquor. A drawing listed twenty-two restricted articles without spirits included. Another correspondent asked what could be done "to stop the increase of drunkenness, indecency and an utter disrespect for God and man," finding unconscionable "the beer traffic have the tires, gasoline, sugar, grains, etc., necessary to carry on their business."

Racism surfaced. A Gallup poll disclosed a different take on the Japanese. The *Evening News* gibed, "Judging by typical Negro newspapers, the way to 'advance' colored people is to teach them to hate white people." John Roy Carlson's *Under Cover* spun a kindred theme, with the chapter "Hitler and Hirohito in Harlem."

Unity needs promoted open-mindedness. Ham Fisher's *Joe Palooka*, under "Common Sense," denied racial tensions and proclaimed national brotherhood. Notwithstanding local newspapers running Black lynchings without editorial comment, Harry F. O'Neill's *Broncho Bill* depicted a Black person rescued from a mob.

The Office of War Information (OWI) urged diversity, and Hollywood followed suit. A local critic considered Dooley Wilson's character in the Colonial's *Casablanca* the "best bit performance in the picture." Leigh Whipper's deferential image in *The Ox-Bow Incident* and Kenneth Spencer's GI role in *Bataan* earned applause.

Draft boards drummed calls for men. Changed eligibilities and reclassifications met requirements for recruits. Summons notified teenagers, husbands, elders and Black people for duty. In January, authorities arrested a deserter and later counted eighteen delinquencies. The New Cumberland military post received recruits.

Rationing enforcement stepped up. Short oil supply constrained gasoline. Aided by police and informers, the OPA executed regulations. Decorative red, white and blue placards clarified a gas station's responsibilities: request a ration booklet prior to fueling, check windows for the appropriate sticker, confirm the vehicle matches the identification on the booklet's front and release petrol for current stamps if sufficient and signed correctly by the motorist. Only stamps separated from the ration book by the attendant met stipulations. The OPA picked some stations for preferred sales to emergency personnel.

Several holding *B* and *C* allotments motored without *B* and *C* markings. The OPA lectured drivers about sticker removal.

Agents cracked down. Prohibitions fell on cruising and pleasure trips. Bans affected engines idling in unoccupied cars and couples meeting in remote locations. Officials discouraged decorating graves and barred parents from weddings, receptions, dances and graduations.

In June, gas ration stringencies disallowed motoring for those with disabilities seeking amusement and those hunting vacation homes. Proscriptions on gas-propelled sailing, charitable event attendance, certain physicians' visits and selected social gatherings went into effect. A river patrol curbed recreational boating. Criticism befell students motoring to school.

Violations brought prosecutions. Authorities held hearings, imposed fines and confiscated ration books.

Lawful driving allowed travel to church, shops, weddings and graduations. Ban revisions permitted apartment seeking, court appearances, funeral presences and residential changes.

In March, the OPA relaxed "Gastoppos" methods and revived a trust system. Litigations dropped off, but nonessential motoring continued. More automobiles appeared. Cars crowded capitol parking. As a consequence, authorities cited 529 drivers in one weekend. Charges accelerated in June. Eighteen arrests occurred near swim facilities. There were 6 Harrisburgers who faced charges for visiting Baltimore's Pimlico Racetrack. For stopping and idling cars in Market Square, 4 persons were arraigned.

Requests for supplements were denied. War gardeners and corporate salesmen went without extra gas.

The OPA restricted commodities. In February, shoe rationing began. Canned fish and meat sales ceased. Schools distributed War Ration Book Number Two. Controls started on additional canned products. Butter sales stopped. Officials rationed meats. Book Two contained lines of blue stamps (points) for processed foodstuffs and red for meat, cheese and fats. The stamps carried A, B, C, D and further markings. Every month the points experienced value changes to adapt to meat grades and supplies.

In April, the OPA detected few price breaches and applauded compliant retailers. Black marketeers, however, infected the program. Agents arrested two Broad Street butchers and interrogated fifteen slaughterhouse employees. The *Telegraph* warned that the illegal activity helped Hitler and "is a serious menace to our country, fighting for its life." Agents cautioned radio shops about requiring overhauls and inspections as conditions for tube purchases.

Tire bootlegging needed attention. The OPA revised rules to halt the practice. It recommended the destruction of unused stamps and planned a campaign to curb the illicit trade. The Rio billed *No Place for a Lady*, screening "a vicious black market in stolen auto tires," and *Eyes of the Underworld*, dramatizing "the vicious activities of organized motor car theft gangs that have sprung into existence since the establishment of war-time restrictions on auto and tire sales."

Despite restraints, the *Evening News* saw benefits. Consumption of unrationed and healthy vegetables augmented diets. Ration points could be stretched, and a budget in the black would be maintained.

The War Production Board (WPB) imposed controls, denying schools permission to buy dry cell batteries for fire alarms and penalizing a builder for appropriating essential stock for property renovation.

The ODT aimed to conserve yet approved a firm's request for a truck purchase. It conducted conversations about rig upkeep. To save gas and tires, the office asked for blinking streetlamps, though accidents could result.

Gasoline shortages demanded service reins. An ODT order impacted deliveries by dairies, bakeries and retailers. Agents eased limits on florists for Memorial Day. Busing eliminated six travel lines. In June, the office planned to support defense workers, requiring buses while prohibiting transportation to the circus.

Hollywood scripted shortfalls. The Rio's *Henry Aldrich Gets Glamour* reflected the gasoline and tire worries when Henry borrows his friend's automobile. The Colonial's *The More the Merrier* parodied a Washington, D.C. housing paucity.

Cutbacks became routine. Cardboard bottlecaps replaced metal tops. Newspapers reduced page numbers and column spaces. The Bell Telephone Company urged short communications. A *Telegraph* public service listed venues curbing fuel use, including public buildings, libraries, historic attractions, parks, churches and USOs.

The city resembled a "Labor Stringency" region. Calls went out for ash men, street workers and stenographers. Women drove trucks and repaired radios. Ads pleaded for females and oldsters. The press added job columns. In January, the OPA outlawed bread slicing to save labor.

Residents mustered for scrap. Tin can collections occupied Thursdays. Manpower shortages and bad weather slowed drives. A June push failed since homeowners had few cans due to rationing, vegetable purchases and victory gardening. Cooking fats possessed value. Nevertheless, collections stood below March and May goals.

The Harrisburg-Dauphin Salvage for Victory Committee wanted women's hose. Rayon, nylon and silk produced gunpowder casings. Calls also sought clothing castoffs, mattresses, cords and ropes.

Officials kicked off a metals campaign in April to construct a cruiser, forenamed the *Dauphin*. The Senate promised a free Saturday show for a pound collection. The drive welcomed old automobiles. A stove, a lift and boiling vessels piled the heap. An Uptown druggist gave free ice cream for dated license plates. After five days, the community had accumulated 467 tons.

Bond crusades energized Harrisburg. Organizers established objectives and requested volunteers. Women manned store and courthouse booths.

Collected tin cans piled into a freight car parked near the Maclay Street Bridge. *From the* Evening News. *Courtesy of PennLive.*

The initial drive gained impetus from United Nations Week. The Carlo Alberto Lodge Number 272, Sons of Italy, made purchases. A Filipino spoke in support. Forum programs rallied backers. The "Buy a Bomber" slogan contributed to sales, as did the notion to "buy a war bond to send Hitler a bomb for his birthday."

Inducements bolstered marketing. A Japanese midget submarine displayed on Market Square attracted purchasers. Reports of executed Doolittle airmen stimulated courthouse sales. The *Evening News* printed order forms for purchase "to strike back at the Japs for the cold-blooded murder," stating, "Purchasing bonds help to slap treacherous little Japs." Bond investments won admission to the Ringling Brothers and Barnum and Bailey Circus, courtesy of the *Telegraph*. As another draw to Market Square, celebrities Bruce Cabot, Robert Preston and Eric Rhodes performed.

For the school year's remainder, students extended efforts. Much energy backed community agendas. Pupils collected silk. Camp Curtin's commandos distributed scrap information. John Harris, hearing of the value of blond hair for weather equipment, donated cuts but wondered about the exclusion of other mops. Junior highs subscribed funds for the Red Cross. All secondary

A Japanese submarine captured at Pearl Harbor exhibited on Market Square to promote bond sales. *From the* Evening News. *Courtesy of PennLive.*

schools solicited blood donors. Youngsters aided bond canvasses. Curtin received honors. Harris gained recognition for "outstanding participation." In June, the *Evening News* announced student bond and stamp sales valued $170,583.

Civic groups educated. The Daughters of the American Revolution heard of war objectives. The Beta Chapter of Beta Sigma discussed synthetic rubber. The Junior Hadassah observed women's defense roles. The Rotary listened to a lecture about electric lighting. The Chamber of Commerce produced a reference for its membership, tallying regional war offices. Alaska's importance informed the Catholic Forum and the Kiwanis Club. The latter bent an ear to a pep talk bidding the country to toughen. A strategy discourse before the Exchange Club claimed air power alone could bring victory. To prepare youth for service, the YMCA volunteered physical education.

Groups likewise served. War victims' relief benefited from the vigils of the Beta Chapter, the Girl Scouts and the Bucknell Alumni Club. Red Cross donations issued from the Business and Professional Women's Club, the Soroptimist Club and the Woman's Christian Temperance Union.

The Keystone Chapter of the National Society of the Daughters of 1812 gathered books for merchant seamen. The Girl Reserve Club did the same for Carlisle's military hospital. The Knights of Columbus, Harrisburg Firemen's Relief Association, American Legion, Quotarians and Business and Professional Women's Club joined bond campaigns. A service flag honored YMCA employees. The Chit Chat Club paid tribute to the WAACs. The Civic Club sponsored dances, and the Masons operated a canteen.

Religionists adhered to fidelities. Ministers bade for prayer once President Roosevelt linked it to the Four Freedoms. The Ohev Sholom Temple supplicated for war-burdened Jews. A Richmond cleric spoke of the Cross's meaning "as a universal symbol of honor, beauty and hope." A convert from socialism believed, for a peaceful world, the Almighty must play a greater role. One pastor advocated for democracy overseas. Methodist women conferred to discuss a Christian's accountability for a fair and lasting peace. A Forum conversation dealt with the import of hope to a believer.

The Red Cross increased services. Classes taught home nursing and nutrition. Nurse recruitment began. Knitters were sought. Promotions bolstered the organization. A Loew's *Pete Smith* short plugged Red Cross first aid. A meeting at the Forum kicked off a fundraiser bannered "BACK UP A FIGHTING MAN." A Malayan refugee and local Greeks acclaimed its work. Film stars Gail Patrick and Gene Lockhart voiced testimonials, as did a British officer. Retailers set up window layouts. A former prisoner of the Japanese aided the drive.

Dollar contributions climbed above quota, but blood donations disappointed. Initially, donors satisfied goals. The Daughters of the American Revolution's presentation of a mobile unit boosted access. The B'nai B'rith Lodge and the Zembo Shrine mustered volunteers. The *Evening News* ran a Blood Donor Honor Roll, publicizing givers from the Capital Bakers, the Redeemer Lutheran Church and the Junior Chamber of Commerce. A female escapee from Nazi anti-Semitism volunteered blood "to keep America's freedom." Artists' posters and druggists' exhibits embellished the drive.

Inducements tried to draw volunteers. The donor service extended hours, gave coffee and appealed, "WHERE'S YOUR PATRIOTISM NOW?" The State's manager, Johnny Rogers, promised free admission for a pint of blood to see *Reveille with Beverly*, a musical comedy.

Still, donations lagged. In April, the *Evening News* broadcasted the blood need and later judged the donations inadequate. In June, the paper regretted as "appalling" Harrisburg's low turnout. An editorial pleaded, "We're not meeting our quota! Don't delay!"

Night dancing on the USO's Reist float boat. *Photograph by Ensminger Studio from the* Harrisburg Telegraph. *Courtesy of PennLive.*

USOs entertained, unfazed by the movie controversy. Soldiers attended Forum concerts and viewed the JCC's Sunday films. The YMCA and the Catholic Club posted program schedules, the last inviting war workers and taking satisfaction of its Sabbath opening. Markers identified USO sites. In June, the Locust Street floating club reopened.

Harrisburg welcomed allies. RAF officer Herbert Priestly spoke to Jewish War Veterans about Nazi raids on London. Mayor Milliken received a letter from Sirdar Dattatraya, attesting to India's loyalty. *Joe Palooka* lavished praise on Allied forces in North Africa. France's verve under brutal German occupation inspired, as did *Casablanca*'s underground leader's singing "La Marseilleise": "drowning out the Nazi chant is one to make the beholder stand up and cheer." A Free French soldier in the city remarked that he bustled "to get back into action with the Allies."

Despite a Gallup poll's report of America's suspicions, Soviets came in for applause. *Captain Yank* pictured a Russian-American meeting and proclaimed the Soviets could "NEVER BE DEFEATED." A *Scorchy Smith* character reacted in surprise when seeing a female Russian pilot. The Rio ran *Moscow Strikes Back*, a documentary of Soviet armies counterattacking. Irina Skariatine, a Russian-born defense worker, told of Russia's "amazing spirit" and its women's great brawn. Some read Davies's *Mission to Moscow*. Albert F. Ceres Jr., a onetime staffer of the U.S. embassy in the Soviet Union, provided diplomatic perspective for the Rotary Club.

In May, Milliken announced a "Tribute to Russia." The next month, the Harrisburg Art Association planned to show Russian graphics. The Reverend J. Thomas Heistand, Saint Stephen's Episcopal dean, arranged to send the Soviets clothing. A February report revealed that the United States had consigned 2.9 million tons of provisions and weapons to Russia.

In March, Colonel Carlos P. Romulo spoke of Bataan before the Executive Club at the Penn Harris. The former aide-de-camp to General MacArthur told of Filipino and American valor. He promised "faith in America shall live there forever." The soldiers looked forward to the U.S. return "when the Stars and Stripes again will wave over the South Pacific land."

The Axis came in for damnation. "LITTLE ADOLF," a poem, belittled, but nothing amused about his regime. The Senate's *Hitler's Children*, from Gregory Ziemers's *Education for Death* publication, exposed Nazi horrors. An editorial classed Germans below the civilized because their submarines, like cobras, assaulted without notice.

America's repugnance for Japan surpassed that for Germany. Americans placed Nippon "completely outside the pale of civilized nations." Demeaning putdowns demonized the Japanese, with some unfit to print. The *Evening News* headlined "Allies Learn Jap Soldier a Curious Little Animal." *Draftie* sketched Japanese people as short-sized, glasses-dependent and buck-toothed. A cartoon amplified Nipponese killers of American airmen. A priest cataloged Japan's crimes against Chinese following Doolittle's mission. Captain Ted W. Lawson, a raid participant, did the same, writing in *Thirty Seconds Over Tokyo* "that the Japs had systematically slaughtered all Chinese who helped us."

The Italians appeared benign. The State's *Chetniks!* depicted German contempt for Mussolini and Italian allies. *Captain Yank* illustrated Nazi officers disparaging Rome's army and referring to an Italian "fool." The *Evening News* explained Italy's desire to leave the war and imputed its dislike of Germany, adding, "The Italian people are a different breed than the Germans or the Japanese." A later editorial favored the Italians as "fundamentally civilized" and possessing "a sense of justice."

Harrisburg Italians demonstrated allegiance. A Carricato changed his name to Carr. A hospital's Latin chef scrapped tin cans.

Italian Lake remains Italian. *Photograph by Christine L.G. Ross.*

The *Telegraph* countered a reader's desire to retag Italian Lake. After designating a bevy of Italy's notables, from Columbus to Garibaldi, the paper remembered loyal Italian Americans and dissented from condemning "all Italians just because one of their number, Bumbling Benito, goes haywire and runs amok."

Barbara June and Beryl Joan Yontz volunteer their Tippy for military duty. *Photograph by Ensminger Studio from the* Harrisburg Telegraph. *Courtesy of PennLive.*

Barking dogs disturbed defense workers' slumber but also served. WAGS or Dogs for Defence Inc., on State Street, recruited hounds for the military. Tippy, an Elmerton Avenue collie, volunteered. More followed. Milliken sacrificed the police department's dobermans, Doby and Blue. Kasco dog food and Purina Dog Chow encouraged enlistments. The latter provided a mail coupon.

Harrisburgers enjoyed the movies. Nationwide audiences reached 90 million each week. Theaters booked patriotism, propaganda, realism and escapism. Stage programs also diverted people. Movie house managers reported necking, but vandalism posed the biggest problem.

Films braced Anglo-American friendship. *In Which We Serve* praised the Royal Navy. *Somewhere in France* described Englishmen escaping Germans.

*The Immortal Sergeant* and *Five Graves to Cairo* illuminated Britain's North African role. *The Commandos Strike at Dawn*, *The Avengers* and *They Raid by Night* depicted forays into enemy-occupied Norway.

Downtown theaters booked resistance. *Chetniks* applauded Yugoslav guerrillas. *Hangmen Also Die* showed Czech partisans at work. The jungle hero combated Nazi intruders in *Tarzan Triumphs*. *At Dawn We Die*, *Casablanca*, *Assignment in Brittany* and *This Land of Mine* starred the French, with the last cameoing a schoolmaster reciting A Declaration of the Rights of Man and of Citizens.

Norwegian resisters received their due in *The Moon Is Down* and *Edge of Darkness*. The former, based on John Steinbeck's novel, ignited controversy over its sympathetic treatment of German soldiers. Nevertheless, a local movie critic ignored the fuss.

Hollywood cultivated Soviet-American ties. The Rio's *Miss V from Moscow* symbolized Allied unity. *The Boy from Stalingrad* gloried child guerrillas.

The State's *Mission to Moscow*, from Davies's book, seethed contention. Dorothy Thompson's column pilloried the film as "phony," a historical falsehood. She charged that "understanding will be distorted, not clarified." Although it was a whitewash of Joseph Stalin's crimes, the *Evening News* thought it should be seen. The *Telegraph* dismissed its propaganda and reminded readers that Russia won victories.

Between Pearl Harbor and early 1943, cinema focused on the East. *Air Force*, *Aerial Gunner* and *Bombardier* gratified Harrisburg's B-17 fondness. *Flight for Freedom* portrayed aircraft carrier pilots in the Pacific. *Corregidor* and *Bataan* rendered the Philippine loss, the last mentioned an example of a platoon's final stand.

Movies empathizing with China narrated Yanks making the Chinese struggle their own. The Colonial's *China Girl* and *China* screened American changeovers to the anti-Japanese cause. The State's *Night Plan from Chungking* dramatized the Sino resistance.

National unity became a preoccupation. The combat films *Bataan* and *Air Force* scripted multiethnic units. The Colonial's *Something to Shout About*, a musical comedy, finished a vaudeville performance with a patriotic number exalting teamwork.

Theaters booked escapist fare. *Slightly Dangerous* ignored the conflict. The *Telegraph* remarked, "In an era of dramatic wartime movies, it provides a most welcome light touch." Noting fans streaming to the musical *Presenting Lily Mars*, the *Evening News* recognized "evidence that theater-goers are tiring of the steady diet of war films."

*Left*: The State theater bills a pro-Russian movie. *From the* Evening News. *Courtesy of PennLive.*

*Right*: A Colonial theater movie bashes the Japanese. *From the* Evening News. *Courtesy of PennLive.*

Documentaries enlightened residents. The Carlisle Field Medical School produced *Doctors at War*. Movie houses exhibited the OWI's *Farmers at War*, showing Lancaster County cultivators at work. In January, Letts on North Second Street retailed films of the North African campaign.

Hollywood tunes imparted patriotism. The Colonial's *Yankee Doodle Dandy* rehashed "Over There." The Senate's *When Johnny Comes Marching Home* ushered "The Yanks Are Coming Again," "We Must Be Vigilant," "One of Us Has Gotta Go" and "This Is Worth Fighting For." The latter theater's "We're All in This Together" from *Hi Buddy* appealed for solidarity. At the Rio, *Cinderella Swings*'s "The Flag Is Still There, Mr. Key" paid tribute to Old Glory.

Downtown movie music tapped the mundane. From *Something to Shout About*, "You'd Be So Nice to Come Home To" longed for a lovers' reunion.

Workers celebrated to "Payday" in *Priorities on Parade*, "On the Old Assembly Line" in *He's My Guy* and "On the Swing Shift" in *Star Spangled Rhythm*. The last introduced the suggestive "I'm Doin' It for Defense." *Stage Door Canteen*'s numbers themed lovemaking ("Rookie and His Rhythm"), romance unstable yet funny ("The Girl I Love to Leave Behind") and amour's endurance ("We Mustn't Say Goodbye"). Perhaps prematurely, the latter inserted, "We'll Be Singing Hallelujah Marching Thru Berlin."

Charmed and allured, Harrisburgers eyed the stars. Burgess Meredith, Erick Rhodes and Gilbert Roland enrolled at the Army Air School. They graduated at Zembo Mosque ceremonies in March. Hearsay hinted the later enrollments of Bruce Cabot, Alan Campbell and Josh Logan. Gene Raymond stopped by in June. The same month, the *Telegraph* printed Betty Grable's cheesecake pin-up.

Aviation captivated locals. Flying Fortress raids against Axis targets blanketed newspapers. Photos of Forts and Grumman Avengers in formation appeared. The press made known the B-17's technical details.

A local pilot flew the *Mary Ann*, the Flying Fortress in *Air Force*. A noted flyer returned to the city for a bond drive. When General Henry H. Arnold, U.S. air chief, visited Harrisburg for an inspection tour, his presence roused front-page attention.

Some believed air power alone would defeat the enemy. This after the *Telegraph* jested a denial that Random House Publishers planned a takeoff concerning the biblical Samson and Delilah titled "Victory through Hair Power." The Senate awaited *Victory through Air Power*, Walt Disney's animation.

Harrisburg credited military value to athletics, but programs experienced cancellation or reduction. District Attorney Carl B. Shelly prohibited Sunday basketball. Gold Glove boxing ended. The Gold Medal Tourney, which included army clubs, limited hoopsters to one class. Difficulties caused the city's withdrawal from a baseball league. Nevertheless, Danny Emanuel, son of William Penn's coach, thought sports aided survival in war, and Nobe Frank wrote a boxer's training shaped one for combat.

In May, the OPA named Harrisburg a global workhouse. Diesel power, railroads and steel companies mixed with capital grounds and military posts.

Carriers hummed with business. The Pennsylvania Railroad increased hiring, banned free rides and transported materials, winning praise. The Harrisburg Railways Company likewise won commendation. Overloaded buses accommodated passengers, forcing many to stand and resulting in a contest to label laggards refusing to move backward. Winner "Mr. U.R. Blockingway" and runner-up "Mr. U.R. Hafbak" pocketed war bonds.

A contributor to industrial productivity. *From the* Evening News. *Courtesy of PennLive.*

Firms obligated the military. Steel expanded plant and raised output. The Harrisburg Dairies, under Washington's authority, supplied milk requirements at Carlisle, New Cumberland and Indiantown Gap. The Hickok works on Ninth and Cumberland Streets produced quality antiaircraft components and gained the navy's thanks.

The war caused failure and shift. A grocer on Second and State lost his business. The eighty-year-old Montgomery and Company, a drayage service, ceased operation but maintained warehouse and storage rentals.

Labor adjusted to wartime. Workers increased hours and workdays, and they gained awards. The American Optical Company earned E emblems. A Harrisburg Steel guard received an E. Employees promised to back the OPA.

Some discontent unfolded. Harrisburg Steel suffered strikes, which forfeited its Navy E. The Harrisburg Gas Company contested a United Mine Workers of America's demand for union rights and wage increases.

Workplace safety was prioritized. As plants hired sweater-garbed females, men's distractions worried management. After the *Evening News* reported more workers' deaths than combat fatalities, an employee died at Central Iron and Steel. A fire slowed production at a Steelton factory. Accidents brought death and injury during May and June.

Helpful tips benefited employees. Women in National Defense Service (WINDS) promoted an outfit as acceptable wear. Antoinette Donnelly advised relaxation at work to calm nerves. She emphasized strength conservation, early bedtime and wise eating. When away from the job, she suggested seeking entertainment, activity and repose. Donnelly wanted women to stop worrying and to schedule physicals. Brandon Walsh's *Little Annie Rooney* portrayed Annie delivering nutritious lunches to a factory. A Nature's Remedy advertisement promised constipated workers regularity.

5

# THE CALL PURSUED

## July 1943–December 1943

With attacks unlikely, Washington relaxed civil defense, but Harrisburg's system remained. The local defense council collected folding cots for casualties. Personnel received poison gas and bomb identification instructions. Officials ordered drills and blackouts. Violations brought fines. One alert found the city's bridge lights burning. Another alert surprised residents. Insurance companies saw an opening. J.K. Kipp and Son, warning of falls, offered liability coverage.

By November, Harrisburg eased air raid regulations. Residents were not indicted for staying outside during practices.

Drills simulated emergencies. A mock evacuation of Nineteenth and Forster Streets uprooted households and removed hundreds to State Street's Lincoln School. Defense forces repulsed imaginary enemies in a Wildwood Park war game. William Howard Day Homes residents trembled at a gas exercise, believing it an Axis raid.

Federal and local authorities partnered. The FBI supplied laboratory expertise. The municipality complied with the army's request to close Walnut Street from Tenth to Cameron for the Signal Corps.

Harrisburg's exertions gained approval, but newspapers pressed residents to embrace responsibilities and appreciate escape from aerial bombing.

Symbolic of a relieved mood, officials carted off decomposed sandbags encircling city hall. Schools dropped war insurance.

Inductions and recruitment picked up. Regular calls went out. By December, prewar fathers got notices. Officials discouraged labor deferments and tracked delinquent reporting. A city board enlisted a conscientious objector dispatched to a work installation. The FBI learned of a Black man annoying women and acting in a suspicious manner, "thinking if he would get himself in trouble he could keep out of the Army."

Recruiters arrived. The navy sought reserve officers, marines, Seabees and WAVES. The Coast Guard welcomed volunteers. The army wanted Women's Army Corps (WACs, formerly WAAC) applicants.

Harrisburg responded. An Ensminger Studio ad aided the Seabees. A musical at Seventh and Radner Streets helped the WAVES, as did a full-page plug in the *Telegraph*. Pomeroy's opened booths for marines and the women's Coast Guard Reserve or SPARs (*Semper Paratus*, Always Ready).

Media aped the drive, sometimes satirically. The comic strip *Thimble Theatre* had Popeye planning naval enlistment. *So Proudly We Hail*, a movie to encourage nursing, might have frightened candidates because it "didn't paint a pretty picture of army nurses' life." The *Telegraph*'s WAC Diary, a cartoon, poked humor at a woman's adaptations to the military grind, and a Downtown theater's *Salute for Three*, a tuneful romance, introduced the gender-reducing "My Wife's a WAAC."

The Merchant Marine recruited. Liberty ship construction and crew casualties compelled replenishment. Theaters ran *Mr. Lucky*, *Action in the North Atlantic* and *Two Tickets to London*, lauding the service.

Responding to army requests, more canines were sent off to train. One ran away, and two died for the country.

Mayor Milliken pledged combat against living costs and black markets. His Conservation Committee mustered publicity. To save fuel, Harrisburg situated gas tanks near municipal offices.

OPA rationing conceded and restricted. Consumers benefited when the register removed slippers and gave war workers additional shoe stamps. Rules made diapers "essential" and eased stove allotments. Florists could rent more vehicles for holiday deliveries. The agency disallowed tie-in sales, such as flashlight buys required to acquire batteries. Coal companies had to take on more than regular customers.

The joy riding ban continued until September. Then, the OPA again probed gas retailers. Agents also investigated *B* and *C* holders about supplemental usage. By October, the agency had shut down a station and punished dealers. Ten convictions resulted from unlawful transactions of coupons pilfered from Mount Joy's ration authority.

Agents restrained illegalities. Stipulations disallowed selling without stamps or sufficient points, as well as purchases with loose stamps or invalid

Recruiting women for the marines at the Armed Forces Induction Station, Fourth and Market Streets. *From the* Evening News. *Courtesy of PennLive.*

coupons. A grocer suffered suspension. A woman met with probation for overdrawing her stamp account. Charges targeted a merchant for depositing deceptive stamp amounts in a bank.

The OPA priced commodities and pursuits. Regulations affected used lubricating oil, hosiery, horsemeat, store deliveries and toast, both buttered and unbuttered. Yard service required payment but no price control. Ceilings covered alarm clocks, restaurants, home security and safety appliances,

The black market serves the Axis. *From the* Evening News. *Courtesy of PennLive.*

anthracite coal, potatoes, turkeys, used articles, recapped tires, householders' goods, New Year's Eve entertainment and various services. Consumers cheered rollbacks on restrictions of seafood, eating places and, just in time for Santa, candy. As a public obligation, newspapers printed lists and tables of price variations.

The ration board found violations. Chestnut Street and Broad Street markets priced meats above the ceiling. Because of overcharges, a Maclay Street grocer had to discontinue rationed fat and meat retails. Stores over-capped eggs. Investigators found restaurant owners failed to publicize ceilings. Milk producers sold illegally outside the city.

Authorities asked women shoppers to be vigilant.

While "There's No Ceiling on Love" melodized regulations, the OPA invited endorsement of a "Home Front Pledge," so "they will agree to pay no more than legal top prices for foods and will not accept rational foods without giving ration points."

The ODT issued permits for vehicles. Truck grants increased city and state fleets. Commercial interests gained allowances. The Dixie Cream and Donut Shop acquired a light truck. The Capitol Busy Company bought four coaches.

Bond and stamp exertions succeeded. Newspapers announced goals and progress. Promotions stimulated sales. The Harrisburg Gas Company's signboard pictured a B-17 watch worded "The More Bonds You Buy—The More Planes Will Fly." For the loan, the *Telegraph* admonished "Buy Bond—Bring 'Em Back." A bond wagon roamed the streets, later teamed by a hut at the courthouse. Theaters booked *What's Buzzin, Cousin*, presenting the ditty "$18.75," a bond's price, and *The Sky's the Limit*, featuring a bond tour. Advertisements added attention. The municipal Kipona donated stamps for prizes. Hoover's gave bonds in a war leaders contest. Bond buying granted free admission at a Loew's movie and the Palestra's boxing.

An army tank occupied the Square. Harrisburg sponsored a parade. Margo, a star in *Behind the Rising Sun*, appeared. The Forum held a soldiers' musical. The press boosted with a cartoon and comics.

Promoters exploited Pearl Harbor and the holidays. Remembering December 7 drew on a Japanese stereotype. Bonds for Christmas became customary. Movie houses ran *The Present with a Future*, in which actress Bette Davis, portraying a serviceman's spouse, "is explaining to the children why their stockings this year have war bonds in them instead of the usual Yule gifts."

Blood donations lagged. Mayor Milliken and George P. Sheaffer, the Red Cross center's director, pleaded for volunteers. Newspapers, a poster and a radio program reiterated the need. *Brothers in Blood* and *Grantland Rice*'s *Sportlight*, two shorts, spotted the appeal. The *Evening News* thought the Colonial's *Guadalcanal Diary* demonstrated "a powerful lesson on the life-saving qualities of blood plasma that should, we hope, triple appointments at the Red Cross blood bank."

The grassroots were tapped. Air raid wardens tramped door to door, and a telephone team sought sign ups. The PTA projected a donor's month, and the YWCA scrounged for contributors. The Jewish USO held a party.

The center concocted angles. Pleas marked Labor Day, Columbus Day, Armistice Day and December 7. Mothers' Days coupled childcare for donors. The center conceived of a doctors' day. In September, contributors received window stickers.

Scrap drives continued. City trucks aided collections. Red Rider and Little Beaver, funnys heroes, backed the paper push. Waste folio and tin cans registered under goals. *Freckles and His Friends* supported the metal campaign, but the November endeavor flopped.

Victory gardens endured. Corn bores and Japanese beetles intruded. Tillers forbore the "nice ladybug" (with a white *V* face). It killed pests. Runaway livestock trampled Cloverly Heights plants. At the Polyclinic Hospital's plots, police shot rats. Looting struck gardeners on Paxton Street and Third and Radnor.

Schools prepared to reopen. Some John Harris teachers worked in plants and skipped summer diversions. They returned to the classroom. The district examined textbooks for "subversive" content and hired substitutes to replace military-bound staff. Administrators planned war programs and defense courses.

Youngsters annoyed adults. Noisy and rambunctious, they kept war workers awake and damaged property. Kids stole garden plants and ran willfully through plots. Boys threw stones at laborers tending Polyclinic crops.

Voluntary activities ran apace. In July, American Legion and Moose bands held concerts, the latter on behalf of WAC recruitment. Along with bond and stamp purchases, Girl Scouts raised money for war-afflicted children and trained "for services as aides on farms, in hospitals and nurseries, playgrounds and recreational centers, Victory gardens, in conservation programs, nutrition, pre-flight aviation and water skills, and for emergency outdoor work." Many wafer sales went unfilled. At the behest of General H.H. Arnold, Boy Scouts joined a countrywide campaign to distribute "Keep 'Em Flying" placards.

Harrisburg reached out to those tending the nation. The Catholic USO commemorated a second year with 2,100 celebrants. It started a Thursday night Swing Shift for defense employees. Moreover, it sponsored a hayride (including hot dogs) and a Navy Day tribute. The center's volunteers readied presents for New Cumberland Army Hospital patients and did "the job of shopping, wrapping and mailing packages for time-rushed service men" during yuletide.

The Reist float boat scheduled variety. It featured harmonica playing, solo singing and dance performances. A luncheon welcomed working women. A

The Pennsylvania Railroad Station's USO becomes a hit, staffed by the Women's Auxiliary of the Pennsylvania Railroad and headed by Mrs. H.H. Pevler. *Photograph by Ensminger S from the* Harrisburg Telegraph. *Courtesy of PennLive.*

musical highlighted an Uncle Sam mimic. The movie *Mystery Sea Raider* filled the bill. In September, the last dance took place.

New facilities appeared. The PRR Station's lounge helped transits. Supervised by Travelers Aid, the women-run canteen offered "chairs, writing desks, and equipment." Unions planned a center at 24 South Fourth Street, providing "the installation of showers, lounge, game room and reading rooms."

Institutions complemented the USOs. The Masons put on a dance that drew hundreds. The YWCA tendered worship. The YMCA slated Sunday swimming.

In October, the Community Chest and War Fund launched a drive for $612,746.77. The Chest budgeted services for servicemen, American prisoners and merchant sailors. The fund was assembled by 650 women.

The Red Cross expanded missions. Military nurses received honors. Recruited "Gray Ladies" ministered "reading to soldiers, writing their letters, doing their errands and shopping, playing cards, singing, and…some work in arts and crafts and other occupational theurapy [*sic*]." The chapter prepared first aid and auto repair courses.

A downtown theater gave a nod to emergency care, running *The Youngest Profession*.

Churches pursued new obligations. Clerics supported Red Cross and Russian aid, dedicated service flags, offered servicemen communion and

SUNDAY - DECEMBER 5, 1943
NATIONAL SERVICE DAY IN THE EVANGELICAL CHURCH

CALENDAR AND ANNOUNCEMENTS

THE MORNING SERVICE will be in honor of all our men and women in National Service. Seventy-seven flags appear in the "Frame of Freedom" representing those who have responded to the call. Six additional flags will be placed this morning by the parents or some relative of the boys thus honored.

THE HONOR ROLL will be called. It is hoped that the family of each service man and woman will be present. Eighty-three CANDLES will be lighted as the roll is called. Men or women in uniform, who are present, will take part in the ceremonies.

THE FIRST GOLD STAR appears on our Service Flag today in honor and reverent memory of PRIVATE KENNETH E. JACOBY, Co. B, 39th Combat Engineers, who was killed in action in Italy, Wednesday, October 13th, 1943. He had previously seen action with the 7th Army in Sicily. His "Buddy", a young man whose home is on Chestnut St., Harrisburg, was beside Kenneth when he was mortally injured. He helped to take him to a hospital tent and was with him when he died. The Jacoby family will be present at the morning service May God graciously bless them and comfort their sorrowing hearts. THE FLOWERS on the Altar are in memory of Private Jacoby.

THE OFFERING this morning goes toward paying for the Christmas packages sent to our boys and girls in the armed services and to The Board of Social Action of the Evangelical Church, which renders a splendid service for 30,000 Evangelical service men and women.

ADMINISTRATIVE COUNCIL meets Tuesday night at 7:45 o'clock.

CHURCH SCHOOL BOARD meets Wednesday night after PRAYER MEETING.

ooOO0OOoo

In remembrance of Private Kenneth E. Jacoby, killed in Italy. *Author's collection.*

honored soldiers. The Park Street Evangelical Church's gold star rite revered Private Kenneth E. Jacoby, who was killed in Italy.

Religious conferences deliberated the Atlantic Charter's ideals. The Market Square Presbyterian Church endorsed missionary programs, regardless of the recipients' belief or race. To safeguard democratic Christianity, a spokesman argued that such domestic problems needed resolution. The Pennsylvania Council of Churches advocated federal anti–poll tax and anti-lynching laws, as well as relief for relocated Japanese Americans. It favored a national peace department and believed a Jewish European departure required urgency.

Ministry confirmed Christianity's rectitude. At the Pine Street Presbyterian Church, the Reverend C. Ralston Smith prophesied the country's forces would be "successful not only because they are well trained and conditioned, but because they are on the right side."

Songs and books spiritualized. Lyricists solemnized "Say a Prayer for the Boys Over There" (from *Hers to Hold* screened at the Senate), "I'll Pray for You," "Army Hymn (A Prayer for Soldiers)" and "Just a Prayer." Colonel Robert L. Scott's *God Is My Co-Pilot* vouched that "Coming in on a Wing and a Prayer" coincided with an actual episode of an airman returning his damaged aircraft aided by godsend. A supplication thankful for escaping Java's Japanese invaders high spotted James Hilton's *The Story of Dr. Wassell*. Blending service and faith, Lieutenant Tom Harmon published *Pilots Also Pray*.

Media mocked the enemy. It made Japanese seem dwarfish, repulsive, myopic and simian. The industry made them out to menace victims, mouth sinister smirks and experience diabolic joy. They were said to be cowardly and deceitful and perpetrated atrocities on Allied airmen, white women and Chinese civilians. The tune "Cowards over Pearl Harbor" scored the immoral and unethical behavior. An ad for *We've Never Been Licked* called the film "America's fighting answer to…every bloody-thirsty Nipponese baby-killer." *Guadalcanal Diary* scripted "thirty-five pejorative references to the Japanese." The *Superman* comic cautioned concerning loyal Japanese Americans in the portrait, but the movie *Salute to the Marines*, placed in the Philippines, perpetuated the demeaning image.

Movies and funnys bashed the Nazis. The Senate's *Captive Wild Woman* alluded to race superiority. The Loew's *Hitler's Madman* recounted Reinhard Heydrich's killing and caricatured Heinrich Himmler. *Draftie* mentioned a concentration camp. Edgar Rice Burroughs's *Tarzan* bested arrogant and perfidious Germans in Africa, while *Donald Duck* pilloried Hitler's picture as "that ugly mug!"

Critics noticed audience's desire to forgo the war. Theaters obliged with escapist fare. The Colonial ran *Stormy Weather*, a musical, and the Senate scheduled *Hit the Ice*, a comedy. The *Telegraph* exclaimed, "War Films Off Local Screens!" as moviegoers chose from *The Constant Nymph*, *Little Old New York* and *Ghosts on the Loose*, "a film that'll get you away from your troubles."

Modern weapons established the tone. Military hardware achieved fame. *Bombardier* signalized B-17s. *Coastal Command* noted Sunderland Flying Boats. The Colonial gave free admission to *Destroyer* for those named John Paul Jones, since a ship of that christening "is the theme of the picture." *Corvette K-225* celebrated another antisubmarine. The State's *Destination Tokyo* portrayed a submarine, and its *Sahara* had a tank as champion.

Soothing music mitigated tensions. The *Evening News* believed music's "mystic agency" diverted physical and mental stresses and became a tonic for the war's oppressive lag. "Rookie Boy Blues," "Left Right" and "The General Jumped at Dawn" harmonized the military.

Lyrical sentimentality remained popular. "From the Lonely One to the Only One," "I'll Wait for You" and "It's Always You" emotionalized respectively separation, longing and fidelity from a girl's perspective. "Kiss Me as Though It Were the Last Time" conveyed loss and melancholy. "I Found a New Baby," sold by J.H. Troup, implied disloyalty and betrayal, while "I Left My Heart at the Stage Door Canteen" suggested romance abroad.

Newspapers exemplified public service. The *Telegraph* added war reports by correspondents John Steinbeck and Ernie Pyle. It started the serials on the Soviet Union and the marines. The issue congratulating the *Telegraph* for war service carried the government's request for reduced advertising to counter the paper shortage. The press responded with fewer pages, shortened columns and digits replacing spelled-out numerals.

Ordinary folks appeared in the papers, with photographs of soldiers' wives and babies. The conflict had a price, and newspapers pictured war dead.

Harrisburgers found literature accessible. Pomeroy's advertised recent titles and a war atlas. The *Telegraph* listed new library holdings, and the librarian stocked maps. Publishers scaled down hardbound and paperback sizes but kept their complete texts.

Wartime need not diminish femininity. To neutralize factory grime and dry skin, lotion cases and lipstick tubes facilitated carry. Sachets substituted for perfumery. Patricia Lindsey recommended a talc application after washing. To endure fewer powder puffs (which required protective compacts), Antoinette Donnelly advised tonic and cream. Pomeroy's merchandised

Sutton Leg Color, "the wonder lotion that looks like sheer nylons." Lindsey thought fragranced soaps would delight war brides.

Deployed military in faraway stations craved correspondence. Promptings tugged the heart. Doris Blake alleged that marines cry when girls fail to write. A full-page ad pressed letters for prisoners of war. Bowman's pleaded, "Don't let them down" and pronounced, "Mail is a munition of war." *Guadalcanal Diary*'s "mail scene," said a film critic, "makes you want to go home and write letters to everyone in Uncle Sam's forces." In *Pilots Also Pray*, Harmon asserted, "If the folks at home could see the difference their letters make for their boys overseas, they would see to it that the boys get a letter every single day."

Black people rallied. Bond buying and recreational services contributed. The Entertainment and Recreation Committee of the Harrisburg–Dauphin County Council of Defense, Colored Division, held a dance at Indiantown Gap.

Forster Street scheduled notables. A. Phillip Randolph, Brotherhood of Sleeping Car Porters leader, spoke. William H. Hastie of Howard University's law program gave a speech.

Harlem and Detroit riots bypassed editorial comment. Harrisburgers appeared to be oblivious to the city and country's racism. Newspapers maintained race classifieds and stereotypic comics. No one challenged Jim

Count Basie and notable Black people support a bond drive at the Zembo Mosque. *From the* Evening News. *Courtesy of PennLive.*

Crow. Dorothy Thompson's *Telegraph* column condemned separate blood banks. The State's *The Ox-Bow Incident* censured lynching. Yet critics made no connection to Black victims, one lamely calling the film a "warning to all lynchers…they might get the wrong men." It did portray a Black person sympathetically, and the Colonial's *Stormy Weather* avoided unflattering images.

Crime and vice disgraced Harrisburg. Police arrested Black youths. White kids gambled. A burglar stole canned goods from a North Sixth Street home. Boys trashed gardens.

Servicemen arrived, becoming perpetrators and prey. A soldier thieved a car. Others dallied with girls in parks. A Gap trooper suffered assault. Another's body turned up behind the Bucket of Blood, a North Seventh Street dive.

Prostitutes and camp followers stalked the streets. Authorities, aided by a Black unit, raided brothels and hotels. Arrests nabbed women on South Dewberry, Verbeke and Primrose Streets. Fox Street's Alfonso Kinsey, nicknamed "Coalpile Shorty," ended up in jail for pimping.

Apprehended women faced fines, exams, hospitalizations and incarcerations. Harrisburg's reputation as "one of the worst cities" rebounded when military officers announced venereal disease dropped in the first half of the year.

Pennant raised in honor of Harrisburg Steel's security award. *Courtesy of the Historic Harrisburg Association.*

Harrisburgers sought understanding for "American's most talked about subject today." The Exchange Club heard juvenile delinquency "is crying for a solution." Judge Robert E. Woodside addressed the issue at Cameron's PTA. The Dauphin County Council of Christian Education created a committee. The State Anti-Saloon League blamed drink. Youngsters twelve to eighteen seemed most susceptible. Indifferent parents, broken families, latch-key kids and misplaced patriotism were culpable.

Movies theatricalized homefront maladies. *Sleepy Lagoon* revealed an industrial community's allure. *High School Girl* favored physical hygiene as a panacea for youth misbehavior. *Crime School* alerted parents to their obligations, and the *Evening News* appended, "It is up to you, Mr. and Mrs. Harrisburger, to take a firm hand before it is too late." The paper characterized *Jive Junction* as "one of the best approaches to the juvenile problem."

In the last months of 1943, industries won laurels. Harrisburg Steel celebrated its guards' reception of the Army E. The firm garnered a security citation from the U.S. Office of Civilian Defense (OCD). The WPB awarded B. Abrams and Sons for its scrap program. Harrisburg Railways received national honors for efficient service. No doubt residents identified with the Senate's *March of Time*'s *Bill Jack vs. Adolf Hitler*, screening a Cleveland corporate recipient of the Army-Navy "E."

By December, the WPB reported heavy expenditures for Harrisburg. To meet obligations, the B.F. Goodrich Silvertown Store at Second and North attached a tire repair and recap station. Harrisburg Steel envisioned extension, cutting into and eliminating portions of Calder, Verbeke and Reily Streets.

Safety concerns and accident studies needed scrutiny. In September, a mishap hurt a steel employee. The next day, a conference at the Penn Harris examined workplace safeguards.

Films forewarned danger. *Swing Shift Mazie* pictured a woman's hair snared in a machine. The *Pete Smith* short *Seventh Column* disclosed shirking's hazardous impacts.

A hunt for farm and factory labor ensued. The United States Corps Crops in city hall's Farm Labor Office recruited for county harvesting. The War Manpower Commission (WMC) oversaw employee shifts from essential to nonessential lines. Business and government sought cooperation to prevent Harrisburg's categorization as a "Group No. 1 labor shortage area," which forfeited federal contracts.

To raise production, the WMC pondered longer hours and more pay. Businessmen could appreciate the Rio's *Good Luck Mr. Yates*, depicting "a rare wartime example of a film in which the protagonist does not leave a defense plant for the military."

Housing shortfalls persisted. City hall authorized building conversions. One project transformed two flats into three. Homes remodeled as tenements. Asbestos wallboard, fire resistant, made way for shelters adjoining garages. Smaller radiators saved metal. Plans anticipated apartments at Thirty-One South Second Street. October's National War Housing Week promoted "Share Your Home," importuning householders to convert dwellings.

Harrisburgers engaged in a bomber bustle. Plans developed to buy a B-17 and tag it "City of Harrisburg." Bowman's propped Flying Fortress drawings, one unloading a bomb stick, to push bonds. The *Evening News* reported Lieutenant William Lotz Jr. soaring his B-17 over the city. Lotz, a Catholic High grad, winged his Curtin Street parents.

The future boded well for Allied air. General Arnold predicted long-range bombers making roundtrips, with U.S. departures to Berlin destinations. The *Evening News* remarked, "The several places we would not care to be in the near future, include the shoes worn by Adolf Hitler." Nobe Frank reminded readers of their comfort and asked them to imagine "Berliners doing that with the threat of giant bombers continually in the mind, and literally always over their heads." Officials promised the new B-29 for Pacific action, with sorties imminent.

Restraint and patriotism marked July Fourth. Church chimes summoned parishioners. Ministers offered worship. The *Telegraph* published a fifty-six-page edition, including artist Norman Rockwell's *Four Freedoms*. Residents rested at home. Nevertheless, Reservoir Park's program attracted thousands.

The war tamed Halloween. A quiet evening of house parties excluded parades. Costumes and floats became casualties.

A homefront mood enlivened Thanksgiving. Columnist Gaynor Maddox outlined holiday fare in *Wartime Food Recipes by Famous Hotel Chefs*. Newspaper interviewees acknowledged their blessings. The *Telegraph* urged partaking in turkey with soldiers. With family members away, a heavy-hearted inclination moderated festivity. People relaxed, clergy preached and Harris and Penn played football. Thankfully, the war's turn to Allied favor ameliorated a somber temper.

Harrisburg prepared a tranquil Yule. Defense workers staggered hours. Shoppers crowded stores. Maddox suggested disposition-raising fruit cakes. The *Telegraph* requested a *Holiday Inn* rerun, which spotlighted Irving Berlin's "White Christmas." "I'll Be Home for Christmas" also conjured pining. Trees commanded high prices, yet supply satisfied demand. A turkey

*Above, left*: James R. Zeiters charges with a toy gun. *Photograph courtesy of James R. Zeiters.*

*Above, right*: Betsy L. Ross pilots a pedal car fighter. *Author's collection.*

*Left*: The author in his naval-style outfit. *Author's collection.*

shortage prevailed. The *Telegraph* reported customers might unknowingly purchase Japanese articles. For defense precautions, the city's Christmas tree went unlit.

Clear skies and low temperature popularized skating. The *Evening News* pleaded for a continual belief in Santa because "Hitler and beasts like him have destroyed many of our fond illusions."

The *Telegraph* noticed a changed attitude. Two years before, Pearl Harbor had dazed and shocked America. Later, Americans understood the conflict's meaning but questioned its trending. This December, the paper declared, "can be observed with a general, well-defined spirit of confidence."

Wartime altered childhood. Adolescents worked on farms. They gathered Victrola records for servicemen and won war stamps in contests. Uptown girls gave a Reel Street party for USO aid. Manufacturers militarized playthings. Pomeroy's advertised make-believe guns and model airplanes. Joe the Motorist's Friend marketed toy ships and plane kits. Kids rode pedal cars shaped like fighters.

Clothing adopted patriotic designs. Parents outfitted youngsters in naval-style garb.

Confinement brought togetherness. Doris Blake claimed the tradition "of fireside games is proving a happy solution of the problem of finding recreation that different age groups can share with mutual satisfaction." Homebound people escaped into Monopoly, Finance, Sorry and Camelot. They revived Flinch, Rock and Pit—card games that were forty years old. Bridge and stamps retained devotees.

6

# SLACK AND PROBLEMS MIXED WITH HOPE

## January 1944–June 1944

Allied victories in Europe and the Pacific turned the tide against the Axis. Still, Harrisburg's civil defense stood vigilant but reduced. Officials scheduled blackouts, conducted exercises, distributed pamphlets and projected field hospitals. A flag displayed forty-three stars for municipal employees. A radio program recognized the city's wartime achievements.

A committee campaigned to save essentials. The Dauphin County Courthouse lost air conditioning when the WPB limited coolant freon, a material needed for Pacific insecticide.

Wartime advantaged city finances. Defense expenditures stayed consistent. Blackouts extinguished streetlights, cutting electricity. Taxes set an all-time high. Residents experienced a cost-of-living jump.

Salvage gathered sundry scrap. The Hoak Dairy participated nationally to restore "slacker" bottles for reuse. The fire department accepted old cloth. Railroad cars at Seventh and Maclay Streets held tin cans.

Wastepaper became a priority. A congressional resolution called it "critical." Collections fell behind, and households remained lax. Mayor Milliken responded angrily to criticism of wastepaper destruction at the North Cameron Street incinerator.

The Red Cross Blood Center's quotas went unmet despite a nursery and special promotions. A disabled donor suggested a Handicap Day with conveyance for the incapacitated. Smith Week, for songstress Kate Smith, invited people with the last name "Smith" to give. A group of patrolmen volunteered. A Gallon Club recorded multiple donations.

Harrisburg patrolmen contribute blood. *From the* Evening News. *Courtesy of PennLive.*

The community sought pledges. Pupils canvassed neighborhoods. Soldiers gave speeches. The *Telegraph* editorialized. The Catholic Women's Club solicited moviegoers at State Street's Penway theater.

Volunteering rose with news of Japanese atrocities and D-Day landings. Patricia Lindsey's column assured female donors of no beauty loss and confirmed nutritional side effects.

Notwithstanding disappointing turnout, the blood center received the Army-Navy E Award. A doctor scarcity curbed operation in June, but between November 9, 1942, and May 31, 1944, the chapter welcomed 33,394 visitors. Unfortunately, donations continued to dwindle.

Harrisburgers engaged bond drives enthusiastically. Holiday purchases lagged, but the Fourth War Loan witnessed schools, PTAs, movie houses, Boy Scouts, newspapers and others involved in the drives. Firefighters bought bonds, as did the Fraternal Order of Eagles, the Kiwanis, the Knights of Columbus and the Harrisburg Rotary Club. Insurance men, the Blue Star Brigade of War Mothers, the women's American Legion Auxiliary and the Harrisburg Chapter of the American Hellenic Educational Progressive Association sold bonds. Scouts offered dog washings and shoeshines for pledges. One peddled a bond to the mayor. A Black woman won a pig for her part. Booths in the city provided buyers with access.

Entertainers joined the push. Movie stars Leslie Brooks and Edgar Buchanan stopped by. WHP's Dick Redmond aired a program accompanied by William Penn's choir. The Harrisburg Symphony Orchestra's Forum concert boosted sales.

Women initiated Bonds for Babies. A purchase on a child's behalf carried the beneficiary's name. A Walt Disney character inscribed certification. Pomeroy's exhibited an honor roll for children. The bonds were invested for education.

A folk festival opened the Fifth Loan Drive. Progress reports followed. Women, employees and YMCA volunteers participated. The Normandy invasion, Flag Day parade and *Telegraph* commentary assisted in the drive. Notable authors arrived to help. Loew's dangled a free movie for a bond purchase.

By June's end, Harrisburg expressed satisfaction as bond buying increased. Residents subscribed to 73 percent of the drive's goal.

Washington wanted men. The supply of qualified men shrunk. Relentless combat spent ranks. Authorities considered inducting the previously excluded, including fathers.

Draft boards called frequently. Officials limited deferments. By March, married men and fathers got notices. In April, three thousand 4-Fs awaited reclassification. In January, the navy enrolled seventeen-year-old radiomen. Three months later, marines accepted recruits of the same age.

The marines wanted dogs. The corps preferred male doberman pinschers and German shepherds, as they were judged adept at jungle fighting. A

Store employees march to a Forum rally for the Fifth War Loan. *Photograph by Ensminger Studio from the* Harrisburg Telegraph. *Courtesy of PennLive.*

A P-40 fighter aids recruiting for Air WACs. *Photograph by Ensminger Studio from the* Harrisburg Telegraph. *Courtesy of PennLive.*

request to deliver fifty canines landed at Dr. Kutz's State Street office. The WAGS recruiter needed to meet a May 25 deadline.

The armed forces wanted women. Harrisburg became a recruiting hub. In January, WACs organized programs and screened *We're in the Army Now*. Pomeroy's held a WAC exhibit accompanied by a P-40 on Market Square.

Theaters cooperated with the effort to bring women into the armed forces. The Senate welcomed recruits to the *Ladies Courageous* premiere, an encomium to female pilots. The short subjects *It's Your War Too* and *To the Ladies* aided the drive, the latter scheduled with Women's Army Corps Recruiting Week of May 11 to 17. Management set recruitment aims, established booths, distributed applications, billed newsreels and flew pennants. A parade and radio program lent support. In May, theater managers agreed to a campaign extension.

Other services pressed for enlistees. WAVES explained its role and training at Edison assemblies. Recruiters pursued volunteers through January. A WAVE traveling squad arrived, installing headquarters in the post office. Milliken announced May as WAVE month. The SPARS created a regional office. The marines sought sign ups at a Pomeroy's booth.

Gallup reported public sanction for images of American war dead. The *Telegraph* published a photograph of casualties lying beside a tank.

The press informed readers of local casualties. Parents learned that their army nurse died in Italy. A service honored Sergeant H. Snook, another Italian death. In April, a city man received wounds at Anzio, a Hill airman went missing and four area soldiers died. June told of another serviceman unaccounted for, a Burmese casualty, a military funeral and fourteen central Pennsylvanians slain.

In January, Washington complimented local OPA boards. Radio recounted how they rationed sugar, rubber, fuel and food. Additional items such as trucks, shoes, butter and typewriters had come under purview.

Gasoline regulations encountered adjustments and disobedience. OCD officials acquired supplements for duties. Others got "personal necessity" increases if withholding inflicted difficulties. Nevertheless, nonessential motoring continued. Tire inspectors checked for wear. *Freckles and His Friends* had a policeman question a car-borne couple with the double entendre, "Are you pleasure driving?"

An Office of War Information radio photo showing dead Americans lying near a tank in Italy. *Picture by W.C. Allen, Associated Press from the* Harrisburg Telegraph. *Courtesy of PennLive.*

Investigations uncovered black markets, including gas sales without coupons, with unendorsed coupons and with counterfeit coupons. Officials indicted a city dealer.

The black market tainted shoes. North Third Street's Schiff Company retailed footwear minus coupons. Officials penalized shoe outlets on Market Street for merchandising without coupons. OPA advisories forbid fake stamps in transactions.

Pricing adapted and fluctuated. Guidelines impacted strawberries, onions, cod, milk, bread, chicken and rabbit, as well as malt and Tom Collins. Ceilings limited the costs of appliances, hose, farm equipment and female fabrics. Rules prevented camera shops from imposing rents as preconditions for purchase. The OPA removed regulations on faddist articles deemed insignificant and unenforceable.

OPA supervision detected violations. Two brothers sold non-graded meats above ceilings. Military police and Shore Patrols checked unlawful charges for servicemen in diners. In March and April, hundreds of district stores priced off levels. For exceeding wholesale ice cream ceilings, the Hershey Creamery Company on South Cameron Street paid a penalty over $81,000.

District director Frank J. Loftus bragged, "The Nation's over-all cost of living had been cut one-third of one per cent." In April, the OPA disclosed prices much lower in 1944 than 1918, World War I's final year.

Harrisburg aided victory gardeners. Dr. Ross chaired a thirty-member committee. The city plowed municipal land for applicants. The OPA allocated fuel supplements under certain conditions. Spokesmen lectured before the Garden Club, the YMCA Men's Club, the Wise Men's Club and the Catholic High and Melrose PTAs.

Comics and songs mirrored tilling. *Little Annie Rooney*'s character prided "a victory garden all my own." *Donald Duck* grumbled about trespassing chickens. The Music War Committee pleaded for more cultivators with a rhymed triplet: "Don't hang around that hotel lobby/Go and plant some fresh kohlrabi/Make your garden work your hobby/We've gotta dig for Victory."

Some plots went unworked. Heavy rains ruined others, but officials saw "progress." Nevertheless, Gallup noticed a "lagging" concern and productive shortfall. Harrisburg admitted as much, confessing an unsuccessful effort.

The school district discharged obligations. Administrators transferred pupil records of those soon to enlist. They set aside sites for military testing. At the WPB's behest, building modifications ceased.

Counting new USOs, Harrisburg numbered six venues and the river barge. John A. Phillips, president of the Pennsylvania Industrial Union Council, congratulated the city. The Penn building, organized to accommodate recreation and entertainment for Black people, coincided with council conviction. Judge Hubert T. Delaney, a prominent New York Black man, observed, "We all know that a house divided against itself cannot stand." He prescribed, "As Americans we must decide to stop giving lip-service to democracy, and make it a living thing."

USOs heeded religion. At South Fourth Street, the Christian Victory Center, backed by York gospels, functioned "for clearing up spiritual problems as well as to provide physical comforts." In May, the YWCA sponsored open house worship. Its trainees heard a speech revealing the USO's theological bent.

Harrisburg's fellowships touted contributions. In 1943, the Locust Street center tallied 23,811 guests. The Elks entertained 85,000. For its initial twenty-one days, the Labor Club pleased 10,000, during which 240 aides volunteered 2,596 hours.

Conniving shortchanged families. The *Telegraph* denounced "a new low in crime and petty thievery." Crooks pilfered "thousands" of dependents' subsidies.

Women fronted voluntary services. *Joe Jinks* sketched a female signing for a USO tour. The PRR installed a travelers' lobby. Once opened, matrons waited on 213,000 visitors. Brooches awarded its volunteers for laboring fifty hours.

For hostesses, Patricia Lindsey formulated appearance and behavior standards. The code included lipstick application, dressing in "soft clothes, and a flower in your hair." She said that a "natural bubbling over type of good spirit" stems from physical activity, nutritional consumption and eight hours of slumber. A "gentle, sweet, sympathetic" demeanor engaging cheery chitchat should exclude "military secrets," she added.

Authorities addressed the venereal plague. Central Iron and Steel aired the problem. The area acknowledged Social Hygiene Day, "providing united community action against social diseases." Infected carriers lost restaurant employment. The Rotary Club heard Josephine D. Abbott, American Social Hygiene Association representative, lecture on susceptible youth.

The Third Service Command applauded the mayor and police for their strides. Disease incidents for Harrisburg dropped 22 percent in early 1943, "the best record in the State." A later report revealed a reduction of over 44 percent from the preceding year.

An editorial questioned race's link to immorality. Newspapers had identified Black prostitutes as "Negro" and gave the impression "that prostitution was a Negro monopoly." Claiming an abundance of white streetwalkers, the opinion piece wanted more raids on their houses.

Harrisburgers digested samples of juvenile mischief, labeled "America's most devastating menace on the home front." WKBO broadcasted the thirteen-week serial *Here's to Youth*, which included adolescent casting. The State ran the *March of Time*'s *Youth in Crisis*, attributing culpability for the behavior to the war. The Rio's *Girls on Probation* pictured a troubled young woman. Youth organizers viewed the Colonial's *Where Are Your Children?*, a drama concerning untoward teens.

When classicist Arthur Rodzinski held "Boogie Woogie" responsible for teen antics, crooner Frank Sinatra barked "Bunk." Bandleader Tommy Dorsey echoed Sinatra, endorsing jitterbug and retorting, "It's those very dancing kids who are beating the Nazis and Japs and its their sense of timing and rhythm that's helped to make them better soldiers."

A Civic Club speaker dwelled on "the menace of increasing tide of racial intolerance." However, Harrisburg dissembled the issue. Camp Curtin scheduled a "Negro Week" program. Integrated church singing accommodated "Race Relations Day." President Roosevelt highlighted the observance since a unified nation contributed to Allied solidarity.

Draft calls shrunk labor. *Telegraph* employment ads increased. Job placements rose. Women constituted over 28 percent of the new jobs.

Makeshifts appeared to offset the labor shortage. The ODT sponsored car care training. The PRR rethought brakemen hours and hired migrant workers from Mexico. The Harrisburg Railways deliberated drivers' qualifying age. Both carriers hired women. In fact, one woman found work as a brakeman. Employers welcomed women at steel plants and liquor stores. Farms engaged women. The *Evening News* prodded them to do their own house painting. The school district issued student work permits. Employment of veterans, some disabled, gained headway.

The *Evening News* suggested prisoners of war might resolve the shortfall.

U.S. Route 22 traffic congested between Harrisburg and Indiantown Gap. A four-lane upgrade from Progress to Harpers Tavern won endorsement. Labor sufficed to start construction in May.

Entering industrial environments demanded female adjustments. Lindsey prescribed cautions. For eyes, she recommended drops, washing, touching, massage lotions and temperature-varied packs. She counseled about lacerations, footwear, insomnia and meals. Lindsey suggested heated beverages and water bottles combined with relaxation. Physical exertion, she added, could relieve constipation.

In January, Harrisburg learned of the Bataan Death March. The country sickened at revelations of Japanese brutalization of American prisoners. West Coasters wanted revenge. Subsequent reports disclosed more atrocities.

Commentary bristled condemnation. Dorothy Thompson wrote, "I felt the gorge rise in my throat, the steel enter into my heart, and horrified bafflement encompass my brain." The *Telegraph* opined, "Americans now know the true nature of their Oriental enemy and are determined to do everything physically possible to speed the annihilation of the Tokio end of the Axis." Lieutenant Harmon believed Washington withheld the "worst" and wondered whether the public could bear the reality. The *Evening News*, recalling the "stories of Jap barbarism," wondered why Americans protested flame throwers.

Visuals evoked enemy viciousness. Defense plants displayed war crimes posters. Loew's billed *Cry Havoc*, a film portraying nurses on Bataan. The *Telegraph* inferred "at the end, one realizes the fate of these women. Not a pretty one—not one that will leave you in a happy frame of mind." The Colonial's *The Purple Heart* depicted the mistreatment of U.S. airmen. The *Evening News* heralded its "propaganda" and assured, "It is certain to make you fighting mad….It will be a long time before the screen matches the striking savagery and brutality."

In April, the Harrisburg Public Library acquired *Ten Escape from Tojo*. Written by veterans, the exposé recounted the Bataan ordeal. The authors attested, "We believe the facts as presented give a fair picture of the enemy we face in the Pacific."

The plight of populations under Axis occupation cried for response. Greek businesses funded the Red Cross. The Engineers Society of Pennsylvania saw a film concerning the Netherlands. A Filipino serviceman spoke to the Rotary. A Korean person appeared before the Lions.

The Jewish community minded coreligionists. The North Third Street center scheduled a speech on the German people's accountability for Nazi atrocities. Jews learned of the American Palestine Committee's votes, asking for Washington's endorsement of a refuge. The Beth El Temple worshipped in honor of victims of Poland's Warsaw uprising.

Mrs. Esti Freud, Sigmund Freud's daughter-in-law, visited Harrisburg. She stayed with retailer Mary Sachs while helping the United Jewish Community of Harrisburg's annual fundraiser. Supported by two hundred aides soliciting house to house, the campaign gathered moneys for Jewish relief.

War-related motion pictures crested in 1943. Nevertheless, 56 percent of Hollywood's productions referenced the conflict. Griping about such content resulted in downtown theaters booking escapism.

A moviegoer's *Telegraph* letter divulged her overhearing a woman's complaint about *The Purple Heart*'s cruelty and her desire for entertainment. The correspondent liked musicals but considered the whine wrongheaded, believing films required realism. "I think what we on the home front need is more movies that make us realize this war is not a bed of roses."

Homefront films focused "a vital story of democracy mobilized for war." The Rio's *There's Something About a Soldier* storied military enlistments and training. The Senate's *Tender Comrade* and the State's *The Doughgirls* exemplified the housing shortage. Defense workers plied in *Broadway Rhythm*, *Gangway for Tomorrow*, *Rosie the Riveter* and *Meet the People*. A band entertained plant labor in *Sweethearts of the U.S.A.*, while soldiers enjoyed performances in *Thousands Cheer*, *Cowboy Canteen* and *Two Girls and a Sailor*. *The Eve of St. Mark* and *Happy Land* pictured notifications of sons lost. The latter envisioned war's impact on one home in an emblematic hamlet. Journalist William Allen White appraised it as a "gift" for America.

Literature gauged the public temper. Readership paralleled national preference. Residents culled novels and nonfiction.

Reviews dotted agendas. The Soroptimist Club heard Gordon S. Seagrave's *Burma Surgeon* summarized. A Beth El gathering examined Carlson's *Under Cover*. Its Sisterhood of the Temple hosted critiques of Betty Smith's *A Tree Grows in Brooklyn* and John P. Marquand's *So Little Time*. The American Association of University Women perused Walter Lippmann's *U.S. Foreign Policy*.

*We Shall Not Forgive* circulated in Harrisburg. Printed by Moscow's Foreign Languages Publishing House, the broadside revealed gruesome images confirming "the horrors of the German invasion."

Songs, many from movies, sentimentalized for those distracted by the war. The "United Nations Hymn" from *Thousands Cheer* honored allies. The *Song of Russia*'s "And Russia Is Her Name" lauded Soviets. *Broadway Rhythm*'s "Brazilian Boogie Woogie" tightened good neighbor knots, and "Milkman, Keep Those Bottles Quiet" acknowledged swing shift strains. *A Guy Named Joe* revived "I'll Get By." *Meet the People* disparaged Hitler as "Shickelgruber." *Hey Rookie*'s "The Streamlined Sheik" humorized boy and girl encounters. *You Can't Ration Love*'s "Nothing Can Replace a Man" conceded the uncertainty of finding romance.

"The World Is Waiting for the Sunrise" and "Make Way for Tomorrow" conjured peace. "Hot Time in the Town of Berlin" assumed victory.

One lyric begged for amity. "The House I Live In" from *Follow the Boys* spirited racial concord.

The *Evening News* defended the nonsensical "Mairzy Doats," a baby-talking ditty. Dismissing the notion of "a dire commentary on our national

Two Fortresses compared. AP Features. *From the* Harrisburg Telegraph. *Courtesy of PennLive.*

state of mind," the paper, reminding readers of World War I's "K-K-K-Katy," believed it "as genuinely inspired a popular song as we have had since the war began" and much more livened than "Goodbye, Momma, I'm Off to Yokohama" and "Say a Prayer for a Pal on Guadalcanal."

Harrisburg commemorated patriotism, intending to offset cultural differences. During Americanization Week, the Junior Chamber of Commerce held a flag dedication. Italian Americans, especially concerned about demonstrating loyalty, planned for "I Am an American Day," with Lodge Carlo Alberto No. 272, Order of Sons of Italy in America, Royal Italian Musical Club, Lodge Qarta Italia, Order of Sons of Italy

Independent and Societá Italiana Indipendente taking part. The affair at Chestnut Street Hall, among newly naturalized, heard Judge J. Paul Rupp speak of protecting liberty.

After festivities, the FBI allowed noncitizens to repossess seized property. The concession applied to Italy's migrants but not Germany's.

B-29s captured attention. The *Telegraph* made a B-17 comparison. The *Evening News* published a photograph and greeted readers with "Japs will soon be getting plenty of U.S. scrap." Despite the air power hullaballoo, General Dwight D. Eisenhower forewarned that ground campaigns would be required for victory.

Some fancied ships. The *Harrisburg*, a World War I troop transport, had been decommissioned. The American Legion's Post No. 27 petitioned Congress for a city-christened cruiser, imparting, "We are not aware that any unit of the United States Navy is now named or is planned to be named Harrisburg."

Girls mailed pin-ups, bonding servicemen to home. Photography adorned calendars, many of sensual belles. Stars Betty Grable and Rita Hayworth beautified foxholes. Grable meant more than eroticism. She charmed "as a symbol of the woman for whom American men—especially American working-class men—were fighting." Her fairness endeared her to white soldiers in the Pacific who were engaged in a vicious conflict. In a country embracing Caucasian primacy, "Grable provided the superior image of American womanhood."

Derry Street's Margie Hazda, a bomber crew's "smile girl" and a Middletown Air Depot employee. *From the* Evening News. *Courtesy of PennLive.*

Grable came to the area. She enjoyed her stay. Surprisingly, her Hershey stopover stirred little notice.

The *Evening News* photographed a bomber crew's adopted lass. Regarded their "smile girl," Derry Street's Margie Hazda inspired requests for larger photos. She personified the one who crewmen liked to behold following a mission.

The city braced for a continental invasion. In January, *Dick Tracy* mentioned a "second front." Churches planned special rites. Stores promised closings for employee worship. Loew's advertised that patrons could pray and would hear bulletins as well as the national anthem. The *Telegraph* anticipated that its editions would be bought up.

On D-Day, the *Evening News* hailed, "Good Evening, Herr Hitler: The Yanks are coming!" Issues sold quickly. Churches offered services, and businesses shut down. President Roosevelt asked for prayer. Municipal council and Harrisburg Steel complied, the latter tacking on a "Battle Hymn of the Republic" vocal. City schools invited clergy to minister programs. Milliken pressed for unimpeded exertion for the duration.

Citizens voiced mixed feelings. Many with folks abroad worried, though several expressed elation.

Placidity prevailed downtown. No rallies occurred. Some hung flags. Residents purchased newspapers. They conversed in buses, on street corners and at eating places.

The war's end seemed near. Once the war was over, Americans desired households and automobiles. Masses might possess televisions. Plastic baths would be available. Prefab homes became a topic. Buyers might be offered furnished houses.

Car manufacturers readied reconversion. The *Evening News* editorial "SPEED BINGE" rued the day of sixty-five-mile-an-hour acceleration and increased mishaps: "When normal driving is resumed, our pent-up desire for speed will lead the country on an awful motoring binge if we are not curbed."

Travel would transform. Aerial advances signified enjoyable cross-country flights. Harrisburg awaited a "helicopter taxicab service." Railroad apparatus would be plastic. Buses might rely on radio to bypass jams and maintain schedules.

Forums considered Berlin's fate. One spokesman feared a Fourth Reich. The YMCA raised the dilemma: "Leniency or Severity with Germany." William B. Ziff predicted a Nazi revival. His *The Gentlemen Talk of Peace* warned of imminent conflict, lamenting "the bitter realization that victory has been torn out of her very grasp, in this brilliant gamble to possess the earth, the Third Reich will move with quiet calculation to prepare for that next phase which is to bring final victory."

7

# PREMATURE RELAXATION

## July 1944–December 1944

German armies suffered repeated setbacks. Western forces liberated Rome and Paris. They approached the Siegfried Line. Russians overran Bulgaria, Romania and Hungary and drove on Poland, threatening East Prussia.

Germany's impending collapse hurried preparation. Mayor Milliken planned restraint "rather than hilarity and pandemonium," including "worship and prayers." Sirens would sound. Off-duty police would report. Milliken anticipated forty-eight hours of rejoicing. Churches scheduled services. A café promised to cease a day's business. The Odd Fellows wanted taverns shut. Governor Edward Martin, requesting calm, would close liquor stores. No added buses would be ordered.

Soothsayers saw victory by December. Sheets sounded the mood and ridiculed the Nazi dictator: "Maybe Hitler now wishes for old paper-hanging job" and "Hitler's theme song, 'Watch the Rhine.' Another recalled an earlier triumph: "Yanks are following in Dad's footsteps." *Tillie the Toiler* punned "Die Wacht am Rhein."

The war's end beckoned. The *Evening News* reveled, "The lights are going on again all over Europe." The American Legion Post band mushroomed "When the Lights Go on Again (All Over the World)." The Civic Club heard a peace lecture.

Many warned of prematurity. The editorial "Watch Your Step" cautioned against indolence, complacency and airy hopes. A "Greetings" counseled, "Don't celebrate yet!" Assuming Germany's defeat, the *Evening News*

The Russian Bear skedaddles a Nazi across the Polish border. *From the* Evening News. *Courtesy of PennLive.*

reckoned, "We must chase a million Japs all over China and slaughter the lot before our job is over." The Kiwanis listened to the Associated Press's E. Norman Lodge assail homefront indifference, saying, "The boys feel strongly about domestic troubles especially strikes." He flayed the mentality "which allows people to cash in War Bonds 60 days after their purchase and the 17 to 20 per cent of persons who make appointments at a blood bank and then do not appear." The *Telegraph* believed peace hopes slowed the scrap paper drive. Relatives of Asian servicemen thought celebrations inappropriate when reading China reports.

Excitement cooled. The *Evening News* detected "less talk about victory in October," confessed "some of our frantic preparations for V-E Day look a little foolish" and confirmed "dreaming about V-Day is at an end." The *Telegraph*'s Nobe Frank labeled claims of Germany's succumbing "just wishful thinking" and affirmed, "The best military minds agreed that there'll be another year of conflict after Germany surrenders." On viewing combat films, Sixth War Loan lenders questioned the notion of a wind-up. A mid-October assessment suggested hostilities until March. A sailor's letter complained of observing European victory while a Pacific war raged. A speaker told the Civic Club, "The Germans will fight to the last man in fear of Allied rule," and a correspondence from Germany howled, "I'm plenty burned up" about *Life*'s publicizing civilians applauding peace. An editorial disputed America's endurance to press Japan once Europe's war ended. *Joe Jinks* criticized complacent civilians. *Little Annie Rooney* had a veteran proclaim, "The job isn't finished yet."

A "Carts Before the Horses" editorial went unheeded. Harrisburg studied a state traffic proposal, envisioning "relief roads" of the "freeway" type. Housing, health, education and flood control made the agenda. M. Brenner and Sons, an automobile dealer, purchased property for extension.

Critics contemplated postwar cinema. *Film Daily* aroused script interest. Films ought to be varied and frivolous, the critics said, like comedies and musicals. It endorsed documentaries and educational films. Social awareness needed to stress "problems, democracy, religious themes, American ideals or international matters." Theater attendance, helped by unregulated gasoline, would be unfazed by television.

International affairs would focus on past errors and current trends. Little countries' independence would be supported. A global organization should exist. The *Evening News* went to bat for the Rio's *Wilson*: "If it be propaganda to dramatize the tragic conflict of 25 years ago, to show its desperate consequences, and to inspire Americans that this time the United States must dedicate itself to making sure another war is impossible, then let it be called propaganda."

Germany's destiny kept popping up. A clergyman thought America should "reeducate Nazis." The Senate ran *The Master Race*, a war drama warning of German racists plotting another conflict, described by *Motion Picture Daily* as very meaningful.

The white man's burden would fade. At the Kiwanis, journalist Don Bate, alerting to Asian unrest, told of multitudes in motion who would resist the West. The white attitude must change, Bate said. He will be forced to forsake Asia "unless he applies the principles of the brotherhood of man, justice and intelligence in his post-war dealings with the Asiatics."

Harrisburg embodied patriotism while relaxing civil precautions. On the Fourth of July, Reservoir Park held a concert. Factories pursued operations.

Plants hummed on Labor Day. A city hall map traced Allied progress. Postings honored service personnel. Milliken noted the air force's inception. The Forum marked Navy Day. The city ended blackout drills and trimmed defensive measures.

Residents could internalize the State's *Janie*, a yarn reflecting community tribulations once the military bivouacked nearby. To handle Gap traffic, the state widened Route 22 by November. To curb disorder, a drinking curfew went into effect. Officials prohibited booze sales to servicemen after 11:00 p.m., excepting Saturday's 12:00 a.m. deadline. Enforced by military police, the regulations barred taprooms from patronage, declaring the area "from North to Reily Streets" and "from Sixth to Seventh, is 'off limit' for white soldiers." Service personnel had to stay out of riverbanks and municipal parks past 11:30 p.m., saving 12:00 a.m. Saturdays. The *Evening News* blasted the curfew as "a dirty deal" biased against the military.

Harrisburgers put up with letdowns. A German submarine sank the tanker *Harrisburg*. Lumber and worker shortages delayed mending of riverbank stairs and slopes. Residents expected food scarcities.

In July, Pomeroy's exhibited how rationing and pricing enhanced purchasing power above World War I. Gallup revealed over 90 percent of the country supported ceilings. Yet black marketing persisted and stood "as one of the most discouraging by products of the war."

In November, the OPA issued electoral guidelines. Voters residing out of district had to find travel means or vote absentee. Campaign managers obtained supplements. Rules for election day gas excluded partisanship. Gas could be purchased if no alternatives availed. Moreover, further fuel could be purchased for transport of the elderly and the feeble.

The OPA governed other commodities. Officials deregulated processed foods, various steaks, imported shoes, used tires and stoves. Housewives acquired more canning sugar. Harrisburg got a higher December tire quota.

Washington bestowed additional pricing authority. The OPA held meetings, discussed rules and posted ceilings. Maximums impacted goods and services. Fruits, cars, plumbing and heating parts, vegetables, meats, Swiss cheese, nuts, clothing, cigarettes, recapped tires, drugs and coal came under control. Agents examined landlord rents and hotel rates.

Repeated violations occurred. Investigators checked and charged meat dealers. Apparel businesses experienced curbs. Agents uncovered cigarette infractions and alleged that wastepaper firms overcharged. Stores failed to follow filing stipulations.

Lodging places ignored rules. Landlords neglected to post rentals, restrain rates and note conditions. The OPA worried about unfair damage and eviction codes. A federal court placed a lid on charges by the Penn Harris.

Other services bore oversight. Prosecutions affected laundries, dyers and window cleaners. Repair costs also came under control.

Walter Young, local OPA manager, foresaw shortages into 1945. Germany's surrender would not alter the outlook. Processed foods, sugar, butter and meats would be scarce. He issued an enlarged catalog, explaining butter's point rise, as well as stricter sugar and meat limits.

Scrap drives disappointed. A public service call set conservation goals and requested kitchen fats. A can campaign in September loaded five rail cars, a "good response." However, households failed to participate. A November push, linked to rag collection, accumulated sixty tons, higher than September but below October.

Paper drives failed. A crucial commodity, paper's value for supply cartons increased after D-Day. In spite of flag-waving appeals, July and August quantities fell under marks. Milliken declared October a paper holiday. An ad placed jointly by firms raised awareness. By month's end, paper amassed sixty-three tons.

Harrisburg scheduled paper campaigning for Pearl Harbor's anniversary. The *Telegraph*'s front page reminded residents of the occasion. Volunteers gathered eighty tons, "one of the largest collections recorded in many months."

Blood donations faltered. North Front Street announced requirements, set quotas, made appeals and tallied contributions. Staff scheduled appointments and accepted walk-ins. Mobile units facilitated donors. The *Evening News* reassured, "Transfusions can be pleasant!" and editorialized, "Give BLOOD." Still, many failed to show. Numbers slacked from June to November.

The blood center reported 248 holiday donations before Christmas. Later, an appeal went out. Under "give one pint more in '44," North Front Street petitioned newcomers and repeaters.

In August, the Community Chest and War Fund targeted $595,319, with under half slated for war prisoners, merchant sailors, USO functions and relief agencies. Officials pressed employees for a day's income.

Reports logged responses. By September, $16,989 had been raised. The amount leaped to $551,411 on October 21. A huge thermometer attached to Sears Roebuck measured proceeds. The fire company used a ladder truck to reach its elongated channel for painting the fund's progress. Scouts, women,

Donald Boone of Forrest Street collected 140 pounds of wastepaper. *From the* Evening News. *Courtesy of PennLive.*

retailers, servicemen and working girls helped the drive. By October 25, the thermometer showed $556,059.

Fanfare accompanied bond marketing. Newspapers tracked quotas. Promotors used prods. Purchasers gained free admission to movies and baseball. Top sellers got excursions to New York. The governor and mayor spoke at "Shot from the Skies," an exhibit of Axis aircraft crowding Market Square. A city policeman bought fifty-dollar denominators for each year of fourteen on the force. Swift and Company employees subscribed above their goal. The *Telegraph* led the state in the push.

At the Forum, a rat, promptly nicknamed "Hitler," frightened females, interrupting a bond performance.

Fifth War Loan quotas fell short. In October, the war finance group prepared for the Sixth. Bond sales dropped and then gushed at city booths in September. The county targeted $12,543,000. *Superman* joined the bond vending jaunt. The Eagles, an association, made purchases. A parade, a football game and movie houses rallied. Downtown theaters sold on Thanksgiving.

By early December, sales reached 62 percent of the goal. A Special Service Star program of companies prompted sales, but they slowed. The push persevered. The Fanny Farmer Candy Shops marketed $100,000 worth. The Harrisburg Air Patrol sold $149,150.

Victory gardens faced adversity. Predators impaired produce. Insects, fowl and critters ravaged vegetation. Purple grackles raided pea plants. Regardless of Japan's Pacific reverses, the *Evening News* quipped, "Jap beetles have made inroads in ever increasing numbers and are being measured by the quart by many victory gardeners and flower lovers." Tillers complained of thefts near the Foose school and the Polyclinic.

Media paid attention. *Bringing Up Father* mentioned victory gardening. The State scheduled *In the Meantime Darling*, scripting a wartime marriage and a "communal" effort.

Reopened schools remained adaptive. A return to the classroom movement hoped to stabilize enrollments. High school shops housed evening defense programs. Faculty revised physical education for pre-induction. Civil Air Patrol cadets received preflight instructions. Scrap and bonds expended energies. Officials framed "Save Lives with War Savings" as a school motif.

The *Telegraph* revered educators of history and geography, believing them slighted and unappreciated. Their instructional difficulty started with Germany's aggression. Map revisions challenged teachers to connect current events to dated textbooks. Makeovers converted "Rumania" to "Romania" and "Jugoslavia" to "Yugoslavia." Japan's capital read "Tokio" or "Tokyo." The *Evening News* concluded that the "war's making most of us better geography students."

Children abided restraints and flag waved. Romper festivity ran without chartered transportation. The Child Welfare Center programed dolls wearing servicemen's outfits with war stamps as awards. Schools received the booklet *Milkweed Goes to War*. Through educators' cooperation, youngsters harvested and bagged the plant, an ingredient for naval life preserves. Children gathered thirty parcels.

The Community Chest reported that school youth surpassed a money goal. The Children's Bureau planned correspondence with military personnel.

Young people engaged in unwholesome frolic. Authorities arrested twenty-five in June. The *Evening News* favored hearings and jailings of "the real culprits—the parents," reproaching them for hauling children on evening jaunts that sprouted misbehavior. In a September piece,

Rampant juvenile delinquency portrayed by Hollywood. *From the* Harrisburg Telegraph. *Courtesy of PennLive.*

"Delinquent Parents," the paper left no doubt about culpability. The same month, the State's *Janie* chided adults for ignoring kids caught up in wartime circumstances.

Hollywood's banner year for delinquency was 1944. The genre intertwined wartime and grown-ups with juvenile delinquency. The Senate's *Youth Runs Wild* portrayed parents inattentive to truancy. The Rio's *Delinquent Daughters* and *Teen Age* exposed troublemakers. The Rio's *Are These Our Parents*, *I Accuse My Parents* and *Faces in the Fog* indicted adults.

Canines reported for duty. An Armistice Day dog show benefited the Elks Canteen. The Sixth War Loan promoted free admission to *Sergeant Mike*, a film championing military dogs. The *Evening News* bet dog haters might rethink, regarding the four-legged "marching side by side with our fighting men, lending a helping hand in the business of routing the enemy." The Senate scheduled *My Pal Wolfe*, a "tender and thrilling drama of too-busy parents, a neglected child, and an almost human member of the Army's K-9 Corps." The *Evening News* applauded Jacksonville, Florida, for forgoing license charges "for K-9 heroes honorable discharged from service."

As churches pursued tasks, a renewed religiosity enthused. Lutherans produced Red Cross articles, honored war mothers and considered veterans' aid. Presbyterians rallied in the Forum. War avoidance inspired the Service Committee of American Friends assemblage at St. Paul's Episcopal Church on Second and Emerald Streets.

Moviegoers viewed the spiritual. *Going My Way* played at the State. The Rio ran Britain's *Men of the Sea*, "aimed at creating a religious atmosphere of sacrifice." At the Colonial, *The Sign of the Cross* portrayed Allied clergy bombing German-held Rome with leaflets as prelude to paralleling "Nazi tyranny and the persecution of believers in Christianity during the days of Nero."

Books themed the religious as "perhaps reflecting people's need for reassurance in tumultuous time." Lloyd C. Douglas's *The Rob* and Franz Werfel's *Song of Bernadette* drew Harrisburgers.

The *Telegraph*, judging from mail, saw an "undisputed wartime increase in the personal interest Service men and women, and their families, invariably display in religion." However, the *Evening News* thought otherwise, reprinting Dr. Bernard Iddings Bell's "Before the Men March Home" from *Harper's Magazine*. Bell doubted the military majority had religious preoccupations and thought the gospel undervalued. He blamed clerics "because churches lacked simplicity, sincerety [*sic*] and sympathy and had compromised with a worldly world."

Mindful of draft calls and casualties, USOs made off-duty akin to home. Volunteers billed regular dances, some special like the Labor Club's Columbus Day, the YWCA's Armistice Day and the North Street's Navy Day. The latter also paid homage to the marines. The Linnekin School of Dancing performed at the Labor Club. The floating boat held vesper services.

Volunteers extended services. Travelers Aid established another stall and offered help at the Labor and PRR clubs. In September, the floating boat closed with worship. Labor Club staffers wrapped soldiers' holiday gifts. A Salvation Army mobile catered to the military on Market Street.

Heads turned toward returnees. The Third Service Command at the Fifteenth Street and By-Pass headquarters contemplated veteran needs. The Forster Street YMCA considered social services. Rehabilitation became an item at Front Street's YMCA, the Kiwanis Club and the Railway Mail Association's Women's Auxiliary.

Jobs became a priority. For the disabled, employment training began. In September, Swift and Company reported hiring. The next month, the State Rehabilitation Bureau arranged interviews.

The Young Men's Christian Association at Front Street, venue for wartime activities. *Photograph by Christine L.G. Ross.*

Other steps eased the homecoming. Front Street donated memberships to veterans. The Pennsylvania Savings and Loan League studied lending under the Servicemen's Readjustment Act (G.I. Bill of Rights).

The Rio's *My Buddy* messaged the homefront. It recalled an Eddie's return from World War I, denial of employment and a veer to criminality. An Irish priest cautioned organizers "that they must plan for the post-WWII period to avoid creating more Eddies."

In November, the Venereal Disease Central Agency of the Harrisburg Sub-District's Third Service Command met. The fight to contain vice intensified. By December, the city's health clinic tested up to fifty women weekly. Combined with regular rounds, the duty meant nurses relinquished lunch and worked evenings.

After Christmas, the state's health department promoted Social Hygiene Day, symbolizing the struggle "in 1945 to control venereal disease and maintain the low rate established this year." The war effort's safeguard compelled a heightened vigil.

Japanese debasement continued unabated. Hideki Tojo, Japan's premier, embodied "oblique-squinted brutality," said the *Evening News*. *Race Riley* recalled "buck-toothed" Nipponese mistreating American prisoners and craving Pacific women. The Rio advertised a *Hara-Kiri* character as a "lust-mad Jap."

The foe was stigmatized with innate deceit. Chief Wahoo metaphorically likened "undertows as treacherous as a Jap with a white flag." Hollywood's *China Sky* depicted a "treacherous Japanese."

Dehumanization followed. The press analogized Japanese to "rats" in island terrain and combat. Colonel Scott's *God Is My Co-Pilot* chaptered

"Rats on the Burma Road" and designated his P-40 the "Old Exterminator." Lieutenant Harmon's *Pilots Also Pray* disparaged the enemy as "evil reptiles" that "should be wiped out completely, once and for all."

Latin America stayed in vogue. The Senate's *Music in Manhattan* featured an "opening number, which is the usual South American type so popular." The State's *Brazil* reflected a "trend in the past few years to capitalize on the popularity of Latin-American music" that "should help cement the good-neighbor policy." The Harrisburg Community Theater invited Mexican PRR employees for parts in *My Sister Eileen*.

But the Rio's *Heroes of the Alamo*, ballyhooed as "wherein 183 Americans willingly gave their lives in defense of liberty," came across "distinctly anti–Latin American in tone."

In 1944, a United Nations concord appeared crucial. Speaking to the Kiwanis, Captain H. Cotton-Minchin warned, "There has never been a more dangerous time nor a time where public disunity between the Allies can prove more beneficial to the Axis than now."

In Harrisburg, congeniality existed among nationalities. A harmonious mixing exemplified the camaraderie of British, Chinese, Russian, French, Latin Americans, African Americans and others in *Hollywood Canteen*.

Jews enrolled in the war and received consideration. The region counted 485 in uniform. Governor Martin praised the Palestinian concept.

Films chronicled the Jewish plight. The State's *Address Unknown* pictured Germany's prewar anti-Semitism. The Colonial's *Mister Skaffington* screened an American's Jewish husband incarcerated by the Nazis. Loew's billed *The Seventh Cross*, portraying concentration camp escapees.

Holocaust monument on Front Street with the Susquehanna River in the background. *Photograph by Christine L.G. Ross.*

Harrisburg learned of massacres that only hinted at their scale. In September, Dorothy Thompson's "Mass Murder, Inc." revealed multitudes at Lublin, Poland. In November, the Soviet's black book claimed 6 million Jews killed.

Occasionally, the press profiled notable Black residents. Nobe Frank's "When the Roll Is Called" detailed Doc Crampton's Republican loyalty. Crampton vice-chaired the Dauphin County Republicans. He established the segregated YMCA and led the all-Black Seventh Ward. He headed the ration board and the Civil

Defense Committee Negro Division. He helped with the Penn building's USO. Moreover, he aided athletic teams burdened by war-shortened finances. Furtively, Crampton performed abortions.

Nationwide riots made racial issues known. In December, Pennsylvania State College's Dr. George E. Simpson forecasted a somber future "unless Negroes are granted greater educational and economic opportunities."

Book sales rose, and Harrisburgers kept tabs on writing. The city was the site for George Palmer Putnam's *Duration*. Putnam, an air force major and Amelia Earhart's former husband, fictionalized Harrisburg Academy's intelligence training. The author spent time there, and "his description of Harrisburg, Front Street, its homes and other parts of the city is true to life and favorable."

Comic strip audiences grew. Funnys recorded more readers than the Normandy landings. The *Telegraph* carried some. Favorites included *Dick Tracy*, *Barnaby*, *Orphan Annie* and *Terry and the Pirates*.

Nobe Frank's column singled out Milton Caniff. His *Terry and the Pirates* informed millions. Frank opined, "Caniff is making an incalculable contribution to the war effort through his cartoon strip," mainly his renditions of the Asian adversary. With comics preferred and "since the Japanese are the villains in Caniff's strip the value of *Terry and the Pirates* in keeping the American populace Jap-conscious while Hitler is being polished off can hardly be estimated." The Navy Department, impressed by Caniff's invention of "a magnetic war device," asked the cartoonist "to give it first look at such conceptions thereafter."

If the comics educated, music placated. J.H. Troup discs of "I'm Getting Lonesome for You" and the film *Atlantic City*'s "I Ain't Got Nobody" melodized loneliness. "After You've Gone," from the latter, and "I Wish We Didn't Have to Say Goodnight" from *Something for the Boys* conjured parting. "I'm Making Believe" dreamed of the imaginable. Fidelity while apart ran through "Lili Marlene" and "Ain't Misbehavin." "Ten Days with Baby," "Hey Bub! Let's Have a Ball" and "A Fellow on a Furlough" suggested fleeting flings.

Concerts were patriotic and spiritual. The floating barge scored "My Own America," "God Bless America" and "We Must Be Vigilant," accompanied by "The Nation's Prayer" and African American hymns. At Reservoir Park, the American Legion band performed "The U.S. Field Artillery" and "The Lord's Prayer."

The military valued music. Nobe Frank requested unused instruments that the army needed. Sorrowfully, America suffered an artistic casualty when

Glenn Miller's aircraft disappeared. Miller entertained troops and starred in movies. In *Orchestra Wives*, his band played the swing tunes "American Patrol" and "Bugle Call Rag." In *Sun Valley Serenade*, the instrumental "In the Mood" moved audiences. "That's Sabotage" and "People Like You and Me" intoned the homefront.

In December, a downtown theater ran *Meet Me in St. Louis*, introducing the nostalgic "Have Yourself a Merry Little Christmas." As with "White Christmas" in 1942 and "I'll Be Home for Christmas" in 1943, the song harkened for the familiar with pensive and melancholic passages.

Wartime spending boosted city firms. In July, Harrisburg Steel bargained a shell order and planned equipment procurement. The WPB gave the Burche Company, on Second and Locust Streets, permits to produce freezers. The Keystone Rug Cleaning Company on North Cameron reported mat restorative requests. The Goetze Welding Company increased hiring.

By September, military contracts in the area amounted to millions for supplies and construction. Every twenty-four hours the Smaller War Plants Corporation (SWPC) lent $1.2 million.

Labor expressed discontent. Despite hearings, the National War Labor Board (NWLB) failed to settle metal trade wages. Truckers walked in August, contesting contracts and pay. Teamsters urged their return. Military officials issued a halt.

Workers struck the Capitol Bus Company over a firing, leaving soldiers aground on city streets. The army brought them transport.

The federal Department of Labor revealed housing complaints. The Harrisburg War Housing Center qualified single women and soldiers for renovations. Officials projected six Fourth Street flats. By summer's end, the city expected to attain dwelling goals and planned to close its housing headquarters. The office had housed one thousand applicants. In December, a realtor noted Harrisburg as fully rented.

Corporations earned accolades. For mishap prevention and bus maintenance, Harrisburg Railways merited applause. For bond support, the Dauphin Deposit Trust Company's president accepted a Minute Man pin. The Army-Navy E banner went to Bausch and Lomb optical and Harrisburg Steel. W.O. Hickok Manufacturing Company on Ninth and Cumberland Streets won attention for speedy "output of precision parts for anti-aircraft guns and Navy ship equipment." Harrisburg Gas gained plaudits for the "extraordinary achievement in establishing and maintaining security protection measures against enemy air raids, fires, sabotage and avoidable accidents."

The United States billeted Axis prisoners. Given the labor shortage, many toiled in camps and on farms. In July, 575 Germans drudged in Pennsylvania, some at Indiantown Gap. One wanted to go home. Hardly any absconded.

Qualms existed. The *Telegraph*'s film reviewer felt *They Live in Fear*'s Nazi youth's conversion to Americanism implausible and unconvincing. Nobe Frank reported that a deployed soldier lamented American women going out with POWs. The columnist asked, "Are any of you girls Guilty?"

Harrisburgers sent social invitations to Italian captives doing farm work in Chambersburg. The Deleo family on Bergman Street welcomed twenty-two. The South Street Diodatos greeted five. Disliking Germans, they wished to aid the Allies.

Veterans scorned "coddled" captives. The American Legion wanted rigid regulations. Nevertheless, Chambersburg's Letterkenny Ordnance Depot defended visits, explaining Washington's endorsement since Italians "no longer are regarded war prisoners and that being on duty with the recognized service unit are entitled to furlough privileges similar to Uncle Sam's army."

In September, the Legion acknowledged Letterkenny, but retired state commander Frank X. Murray asserted that the response failed to revise the veterans' position: "We are definitely on record and we believe that any privileges, wining and dining and tours must be eliminated."

The blue sky beckoned. Residents exalted winging. Newspapers related bombing raids and aerial affairs. The *Evening News* joked, "Superforts give Japs different type of scrap." A Muench Street defense unit viewed *Army*

A P-47 fighter displayed at the Middletown Air Depot. *From the* Harrisburg Telegraph. *Courtesy of PennLive.*

*Air Forces Report*, a film narrating the air corps. The *Telegraph* published a P-47's photo at Middletown. Comic strips illustrated aircraft.

Piloting provoked interest and doubt. The Penn Harris Airport gave lessons. The *Evening News* dismissed the "claim that practically anybody can learn to fly a small new civilian plane in five hours." Besides, "if we didn't know that an airplane doesn't have to be backed out of a driveway or squeezed into a parking space between two other planes we'd be a lot more impressed."

Holiday preparations began in mid-October. A city Christmas tree would be lighted, assuming an end to the electric ban. In November, the Conserve Critical Resources Committee disclosed that the Office of War Utilities asked Harrisburg to maintain light prohibition.

Then before Christmas, headlines reported the Ardennes offensive. Two

*Left*: Harrisburg's sixty-three-foot Christmas tree on Market Square, decorated with colored balls but unilluminated to save electricity. *From the* Evening News. *Courtesy of PennLive.*

*Opposite*: Poor-quality view of German troops advancing past dead Americans in the Ardennes. Taken from captured German film. *From the* Evening News. *Courtesy of PennLive*.

days after December 25, the *Evening News* showed American dead. The Nazis, wrote Nobe Frank, "had a sobering affect [sic] on any Christmas celebration," with the Wehrmacht drive clocked "to take the spark out of Christmas." Nonetheless, Frank thought the assault might backfire because it "gave to all Americans the feeling that the war is not yet over—that many difficult days lie ahead."

*8*

# NEAR THE END

## January 1945–May 1945

The Allies pressed the Axis. Western armies forced a German withdrawal from the Bulge and pressured the Wehrmacht in Italy. The Red Army advanced on Poland and menaced Germany. In the Pacific, General MacArthur's forces landed on Luzon. The navy prepared to invade Iwo Jima.

Victory's assurance slackened sacrifice when shortages existed. Workers switched to civilian employment. A demand persisted for nurses. Coal, meat and canned goods remained scarce, as were munitions. The WPB reduced vehicle and tire allocations. Wavering worried Washington.

Triumph's promise prevailed. A Bowman's ad "Peace in '45" showed a mother embracing her soldier son and hoping "that our boys come back to us safely, victoriously...early in '45." *Broncho Bill* characters hailed "HAPPY NEW YEAR, FOLKS! WITH VICTORY IN 1945."

However, newspapers dispelled the mood. The *Evening News* foresaw "a year of hard tasks and fatal action" and forewarned that "we are still fighting bitterly with two desperate enemies whose strength and determination are by no means exhausted." Predicting "the heaviest casualties," the paper anticipated a painstaking exertion "to guard against impatience and discouragement and war weariness." The *Telegraph* shattered the "last vestiges of complacency or over-optimism," denounced home apathy, wanted greater sacrifice and protested racial discord.

Movies awakened the nonchalant. *Brought to Action*, a documentary, displayed "an insight into the kind of enemy we are fighting in the Jap and how far away we are from our ultimate goal, the Japanese home islands." *Objective Burma* revealed the foe's cruelty and confirmed "if the film achieves nothing else, it will at least have accented that complacency should have no place in our dealings with the Nips."

Most residents admitted few wartime sacrifices. Their lives remained undisturbed. A correspondent scorned greedy self-seekers, urging empathy for occupied peoples. Amid plans to celebrate V-Day, a Forum audience heard Francis P. Matthews, the National War Fund's vice-president, state that whiners "would be ashamed to complain about any discomforts if they could see the hardships endured by soldiers abroad."

Postwar musings teemed. Officials prioritized programs. Employment, aviation, railroads, lumber and retailing received attention. Catholic women pondered poverty. Cameron's PTA considered education. Some mediated on marriage and motoring.

Comic strips concerned the aftermath. *Freckles and His Friends* spoke of retailers' requirement to satisfy consumers. *Barnaby* alluded to industrial expansion and "reconverted" plants.

Corporations tantalized cravings. The PPL envisioned a bond-financed home across from a soldier and his wife lolling on grass. Looking forward, they dreamed, "We'll build a house on a hilltop." The Harrisburg Gas Company pledged a "New Freedom Gas Kitchen!" using "GAS the Wonder Flame."

In April, the Rio ran *Sun Valley Serenade*, a 1941 release, telling of a refugee girl's adoption. The film's songs included one touching the city's inclination, "The World Is Waiting to Waltz Again."

Harrisburg endured irritations. Market Square's heavy traffic congested buses. Waiting riders blocked store entrances, angering retailers. Limited manpower hampered ash collection and firefighting. A mud pileup due to bad weather, labor shortfall and material deficiency blocked access to Jefferson Village's Uptown residences, preventing police, fire and delivery services.

Walkouts erupted in March. Maintenance men struck Harrisburg Railways and paraded downtown. Mayor Milliken rebuked striking ash men, ordering them to report to work. He threatened to give their names to the WMC.

Shortages curbed consumables. Metal scantiness stopped lawn mower manufacture. The ODT announced a vehicle accessories dearth. The press reported limited window screens and paintbrushes. Harrisburg discovered coffee hoarding. *Oaky Doaks* pictured a character regretting a dress lost in a flying machine, a reference to apparel shortfalls. *Thimble Theater* referred to

Without a bus terminal, crowded sidewalks block business entrances on Second Street just off Market Square. *From the* Evening News. *Courtesy of PennLive.*

the depletion of beef. Easter shoppers crowded stores despite understocked meat and fowl.

Manpower and material pressures decreased services. An ad spotlighting a child warned, "There's a Doctor Shortage" and encouraged patients to conserve "your doctor's precious time" by purchasing drugstore remedies. Under staff restraints, the Harrisburg Gas Company instructed homeowners to read meters and postcard measures. Pealer's Flowers prioritized Easter corsage delivery to military personnel.

The state's manpower office deemed the Lancaster-Harrisburg-York region "vital" for industry and labor. The government intended to conscript the non-drafted and nonessential employees unless they secured defense jobs. The WMC mustered local workers, veering them to essential trades. In February, businesses promised to yield sixty-three people. The WMC mandated hotel staff reductions. Seven in the city complied. By March, the agency had gathered near three hundred individuals.

The press resonated the crisis. The *Telegraph* echoed the urgency. Railroads craved labor. The military sought nurses. Classified columns increased in number and cautioned women to retain essential employment. The *Evening News* added classifieds and solicited women and locals for West Coast naval yards.

Victory gardens rated greater import. Output ran above goals and had to stay high. Bolstering the food supply offset produce and labor deficits.

Foreign exports strained stores. The *Evening News* intimated, "Persons who have not yet made the acquaintance of rake and hoe during the past few years could well afford to do so now." The Harrisburg Victory Garden Committee formed in March. Dr. Ross, anticipating a vegetable shortage, recalled, "Grow all you can, eat all you can, and can what you can't."

The municipality issued a caution: Cultivators could not draw water from fire hydrants.

From winter to spring, Harrisburg schools backed the war. They joined the Community Chest and War Fund drive and entered a Red Cross campaign. At Camp Curtin, a playing card collection surpassed its goal.

The district accommodated the military. John Harris and William Penn advanced graduation so that potential draftees could participate. In March, twenty-three graduated from Penn. Eleven worked in defense. Four chose war-related college studies. The high schools sited Army Specialized Training Reserve exams. Educators expected Germany's collapse. In March, they requested the city's victory ceremony be confined "to memorial services for those who made the supreme sacrifice and the invocation of divine blessing upon those who continued to be engaged in the battles for freedom." The conflict took the lives of forty-seven students. Over eight hundred still served.

The war revised curriculum. Graduation units rose, adding tenth grade mathematics and eleventh year American history. A math program prepared John Harris nursing prospects.

Material shortages required salvaging. Awareness and fervor waned. Homeowners ignored efforts, which "by this time…should be automatic." An April can campaign disappointed. The amount filled a mere two railroad cars.

Paper remained valuable. Still "the No. 1 critically needed material," it manufactured foodstuff boxes, blood plasma bags and ordnance safety rings. Discarded Christmas wrappings failed a January drive. The Society of the Twenty-Eighth Division spearheaded the next campaign. With junk dealers and young boys assisting, a record-breaking one hundred tons stacked up. The *Evening News* complained of "lotteries" misuse of paper. A salvaging council in *Little Annie Rooney* set an example for adults. But a paper push in April fell flat.

Europe's liberation produced refugees. The crisis cried for amelioration. The United National Clothing Collection for War Relief organized with the slogan "Out of Our Plenty, We Can Perform a Humble Act of Charity." Educators and youth mobilized. Radio, newspapers and theaters advertised. The campaign scheduled door-to-door solicitations.

The mayor declared April 21 a collection day. Boy Scouts helped, and Kiwanians endorsed it. Clubs staged members unclothing as make-believe giveaways. Girl Scouts advocated donations. By April 23, the push had accumulated over three hundred tons.

Harrisburg cooperated with resource management. To conserve fuel, a countrywide brownout began on February 1. The WPB ordered illuminative curbs for ads and displays, darkening marquees, streets and signs but omitting roadway guideposts, physicians' dwellings and lodging places. Also excepted were "porch and entrance lighting for private residents, outdoor lighting for children's playgrounds, such as ice skating rinks, and other recreational activities, gasoline stations, parking lots, and fruit and vegetable markets." Restrictions spared posts providing medical care, police protection and firefighting. Loew's sought an innovative marquee that radiated reduced energy. The *Telegraph* questioned "inconvenience" contrasted to conditions troops faced.

The city welcomed a February 26 energy-saving curfew. Regulations barring liquor sales to servicemen after 11:30 p.m. discriminated by not

Troop 15 Boy Scouts of the Beth El Temple collect clothing. *From the* Evening News. *Courtesy of PennLive.*

applying to others. Now, the WMC's Tri-County Advisory Committee administered midnight closings despite business resentment. Firms obeyed, and the police promised enforcement. A later ruling allowed nonalcoholic service open beyond 12:00 a.m.

At the police ball, a loudspeaker cautioned about lights going off as midnight approached. When the band finished at 11:57 p.m., the dance floor held four twosomes.

Battlefield victories and V-E expectations lessened blood donations. Turnout remained low. Booking went unkept. A *Joe Jinks* character confessed to an "appointment once, but something came up."

Bond calls countermanded slack. City and county over-subscribed the Sixth War Loan. Afterward, volunteers knocked on doors for more sales. The American Legion sold $64,000 worth. Newspaper carriers joined to finance a landing craft. Pitches exploited Lincoln's birthday and Berlin's capture, the latter imploring, "KEEP ON BUYING BONDS TILL IT'S OVER, OVER THERE!" Another discouraged redemption: "Before you decide to cash that War Bond—wait a minute....Don't cut off your own nose. Hang on to your War Bond."

The Pennsylvania War Finance Committee's payroll units prepared for December 7. Beginning on May 14, Dauphin County aimed for $5,772,000. Businesses organized the Mighty Seventh Invasion Plan, introducing "B-Day."

Rallies activated workers. Railroads and industries participated. Hoping for payroll program enlistments, firms heard a former American prisoner. The Chestnut Street Auditorium housed a PPL throng. A Filipino clarinetist, performing for the loan at the Zembo Mosque, probably realized its value when hearing of American landings at Luzon's Lingayen Bay, near his home in Urdanate.

Advertisements incited the drive. One blazoned the "MIGHTY 7TH WAR LOAN." The Harrisburg Gas Company forwarded an employee's ad, stating, "THE BOND TODAY IS A BOMBS AWAY." Morris Square Deal Jeweler reminded, "IT'S OVER IN EUROPE....But we have a War in the Pacific to win."

Show business weighed in. The Rio staged *The Favor* and screened *Leave It to Blondie*, in which the Bumsteads bought bonds despite budgetary restraints. Loew's scheduled *Between Two Women*, portraying a kiss bonded at $100,000. In concert with Hollywood, the Penn Harris hosted Henry L. Marshall's composition, "It's the Seventh."

The OPA carried on, enjoying public approval, notwithstanding defiant acts. Officials ruled effectively. Manager Young praised the OPA's volunteers.

The East Harrisburg Post of the Veterans of Foreign Wars applauded its service. Young commended automobile pools for setting examples. They relieved crowded buses, saved gasoline and conserved rubber.

Young pursued violators of fuel rules. Guy Miscia, a Cameron and Paxtang Streets service station operator, racketeered. Dealers transacted counterfeit stamps. Martin S. Keim at Cameron and Herr shut down until March. Glen Moharter on Market Street and Miller's Service Station at Tenth and Paxton faced censure. The Parkview Garage closed, and Abe Fortune's operation on Cameron and Herr ceased trade. The OPA suspended twenty-two dealerships before war's end.

Meat came in for increased regulations and more stringent control. Agents charged North Third Street's National Toddle House with ration overdraws, ordering it closed for seven days. Officials seized 16,173,809 red coupons held by abattoirs to prevent sales exclusive of rationing. Young "applauded the confiscation as a master stroke against a potential black market in meat in gigantic proportions."

The OPA protected other commodities. Market Street's Henry's shoes had to defer sales for stock and ration inconsistency. The White Dove Products Company and the Harrisburg Grocery Company delivered sugar without demanding rationed cash. Agents withheld sugar from the Goodwill Restaurant at Sixth and Calder for thirty days because of purchases without stamps. Moreover, the Harrisburg Hide and Rendering Company committed illegal withdraws of its ration balance and neglected to give up surplus coupons.

With rubber tight, the OPA cut tire allocations, stating it "should convince all motorists they should be sure of expert tire care." V.D. Leisure's repair shop peddled a flag-waving but self-serving message of a "Patriotic Duty to Recap," the advice of the agency. The garage predicted the tire shortage would last a year.

Motoring regulations were updated. In March, gasoline increased for public and private services. Officials explained ration book and record adjustment due to the state's new drivers' permits. Warnings went out about the invalidation of certain coupon categories. Young reported that *A* and *B* holders would receive supplements if V-E Day increased supplies.

Leasing came in for scrutiny. The OPA allowed rental hikes for renovations, warning new leases required approval. Homeowners letting rooms fell under supervision. Lessees complaining of overpayment had to prove "gouging." The office considered augmented payments for upgraded properties with charges unchanged since the war.

Officials filed injunctions against the Penn Harris. A Reily Street residence suffered fines. The agency ordered overcharges refunded.

Regulations impacted additional services. Cleaners and pressers required ceilings on "men's wear, suits, trousers, heavy and light overcoats, women's suits, dresses, blouses, jackets, skirts, sweaters, heavy and light coats." Workshops mending agricultural gear, home devices and motor vehicles submitted to edicts. The agency checked fabric providers "that own, launder and rent to hotels, restaurants, barber shops, and others who furnish linen for uniforms, aprons, towels, sheets, and table cloths."

Officials asked courts to force Harrisburg's Baughman's Van Services to divulge pricing and sought action against the Maple Grove Café for overcharges. Further, they denied eating places higher ceilings to counter expenses for renovation, fresh décor and entertainment.

The OPA restrained costs. Controls landed on clothing, hides, wastepaper, wood, steel cases, used cars and light products. Agents filed injunctions against South Cameron Street's Hervitz Packing Company (hides), North Sixth Street's Rubin Brothers Company (wastepaper) and lamp firms. In a case, an offender received a tie-in sales penalty.

Oversight monitored food. Ceilings affected meats, candy, beverages, eggs, milk and produce. Fines hit Chestnut Street's Thrift Wholesale Company for overpriced chocolates and Calder Street's W. and L. Beer Distributors for above-limit drinks. Retailers paid damages for excessive banana charges in markets. Investigators alleged Market Street's Superior Stores Company exceeded the egg lid. In February, injunctions blocked four dairies from buying milk wholesale beyond the maximum.

The next month, the government imposed the most stringent controls on meats and canned commodities, extending to vegetables. Agents inspected regional prices. In May, a sixty-three-cent cap tagged strawberries.

Downplaying inflation consequences, the OPA lapsed some restrictions. In February, removals included "sleigh bells, miniature furniture used as containers for flowers, cigarettes and candy; hand fans; artificial or preserved grass and flowers; safety air-vents for wine fermentation; bird cages; wire forms for floral wreaths; dog and cat beds; and alummum [*sic*] horse shoes."

Residents personalized scarcity's mischances and malaise. A motorist locked out of his running car sulked at the fuel loss. Reported coffee wanting prompted Young to dissuade panic purchases. A woman fretted the lack of linens, wash wares and cloth pegs. Young also reassured consumers that stored butter remained untainted.

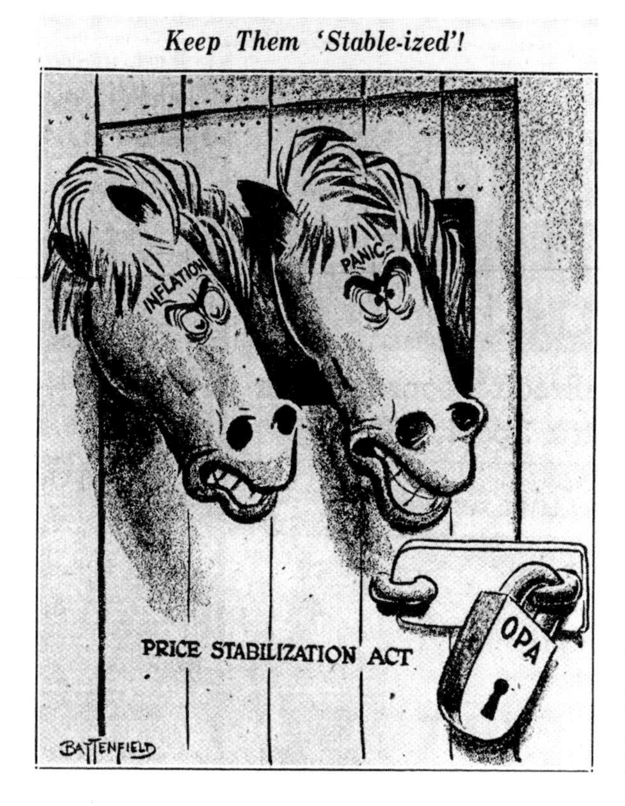


The Office of Price Administration maintains the effort to control the cost of living. *From the* Evening News. *Courtesy of PennLive.*

Regardless, the OPA hedged inflation. From 1943 to August 1945, prices increased a mere 0.15 percent.

The Red Cross appealed for volunteers. Requests went out for nurses, social workers, nurses' aides, seamsters, stitchers and field staff. Members planned an induction center canteen. They collected clothing, made articles and instructed aides. The Harrisburg chapter gave the city library a book listing the Office of Censorship approved readings for American captives.

In February, the Red Cross War Fund campaigned for $372,000. The municipality readied. Meetings took place. Companies and workers fixed goals. Cross staffers requested store windows for exhibits.

Retailers pitched in. On March 6, Pomeroy's opened late, "So That the Entire Store Can Be Organized for the Red Cross Drive," emphasizing "Pomeroy's Goes All-Out." An ad featured comedian Bob Hope testifying, "Folks, THE RED CROSS DESERVES YOUR HELP I know! I saw!" Businesses displayed President Roosevelt's photograph.

Marine colonel David M. Shoup lent support. A Congressional Medal of Honor recipient, he spoke at a rally.

Theaters worked together, overseeing two counties. They screened actress Ingrid Bergman's short publicizing Red Cross activism. Hollywood advertised "RED CROSS WEEK," asserting "Keep Your Red Cross at His Side!" Reports put the Senate ahead in fundraising.

A Red Cross executive detailed its foreign services. A Philippine official honored Harrisburg's chapter, remarking, "We shall forever be grateful to the American women who made the clothing that now covers the bodies of thousands of Filipino women and children."

In the Third Service Command, Harrisburg led WAC recruiting. The city sent twenty-two women to training and intensified enrollment. The Rio's *A WAVE, a WAC and a Marine* recognized the calling. The WAC used "Blue Angels for Purple Hearts" as a catchphrase, an endearment of American wounded. Theaters ran the U.S. Army Signal Corps' *To the Ladies*. WACs accompanied showings to distribute information. Milliken extended congratulations and declared February 27 Blue Angels Day. A parade complimented recruits.

Near the Fourth and Walnut Streets parade route, a man rued, "First thing you know, they'll take all the girls." A woman scowled, "They've already taken all the MEN."

By chance, recruiters got a lift from movie houses. At Loew's, *Keep Your Powder Dry* saluted the WACs. The Colonial's *Here Come the WAVES* not only honored the service but also "stresses the vital role the WAVES are playing in the war effort, as well as making a plea for more recruits."

The military liked Harrisburg's canines. Since WAGS began in February 1943, Dr. H.C. Kutz had sent forty-six dogs to centers. Blue returned from the South Pacific and refreshed at a "fatigue" installation.

Dogs embodied service and feeling. Deployed globally, canine "were workers and warriors; they were soldiers' comrades-in-arms and companions in battle." Scripts personalized ties. A Labor USO playlet affected the "Dog with the Human Mind." The State's *Practically Yours* portrayed a pilot diving on the enemy and crying out for his pooch.

Notwithstanding pending victory, USOs maintained activities. Travelers Aid gave directions and booked lodgings. It moved from South Fourth Street to Fourth and Chestnut to access rail passengers. Local girls attended Gap parties. High school students preformed at the Labor Club. The latter prepared a military wedding in the YWCA.

The USOs provided nonalcoholic enjoyment. When Eddie L. Banks's Alcazar Hotel applied for a liquor permit, homeowners on Sixth and Boas Streets and the USO Citizens' Advisory Council complained. The Boas

Blue Dobie, honorably discharged, pictured with city police sergeant D. Edward Carmichael. *From the* Evening News. *Courtesy of PennLive.*

Street hotel neared the African American Penn-USO Club at Seventh. Residents backed the council, believing too many bars operated and wishing closures instead.

In April, Harrisburg celebrated Army Day. Invitations welcomed citizens to the Forum. Military films, Carlisle's medical band and generals' speechifying highlighted the occasion.

Radio aired appreciation. WHP's Dick Redmond dedicated the daily *America in Action* as tribute.

Veterans returned in need. The Jewish War Veterans entertained some. The State's *Winged Victory* raised money for Army Emergency Relief. Employment opportunities attracted consideration. Radio and banks explained the GI Bill.

The discharged organized. Catholics prepared an association. In March, the American Veterans of World War II or "AmVets" met at the YMCA, inviting men and women uniformed since September 16, 1940.

The returnees required understanding. The *Telegraph*'s "Civilian Neurosis" suggested mothers must avoid "coddling." Your son had attained manhood; therefore, relate to him as such, the paper advised. Your management should not undermine his individuality and "his wanting to do things his way."

Mental problems unhinged a few. Hollywood's depictions reached Harrisburg. Loew's billed *I'll Be Seeing You*, the initial release "to give attention to the return of a psychoneurotic serviceman to civilian life." The Rio's *Identity Unknown* described a soldier's amnesic distress, applauded as a "timely film about a subject that concerns friends and relatives of every GI who's been wounded or killed in this war."

Ads reflected soldiers' dreams. Ensminger Studio illustrated a home bound's anticipated reunion with his mother. Wilsbach Distributors pictured a returned veteran in a chair with shoes off, shirt top open and book resting on the floor.

Harrisburgers responded to Jewish adversity. Oscar Janowsky, historian and author, spoke of the urgency. The Harrisburg chapter of Hadassah, allied with Hadassah's Youth Aliyah, labored to liberate Jewish youngsters and move them to Palestine. In March, the JCC heard a representative of the Jewish National Fund, an organization accumulating funds for a Middle Eastern refuge.

In January, the Senate's *Mr. Emmanuel* depicted an elderly Jew's perilous quest to Germany, inquiring about a victim of oppression. The theater promised a refund "If This Picture Doesn't Make You MAD!" and thought bigots would despise the film, but others would be angered at "the world villains of hate and prejudice and intolerance."

In April, anti-Semitism reared in Harrisburg. A state legislative committee "publicly censured" West Shore publisher A.O. Vorse for printing a letter uttering "unfounded, unfair, and un-American attacks upon members of the Jewish race."

Three years before, the OWI noted the national affliction, earmarked "Group Attitudes and prejudices in the War Effort—Anti-Semitism."

In May, Loew's ran a revelation, showing U.S. Army footage of extermination camps "that offer horrifying proof of Nazi bestiality."

The battling Philippines inspired. *Lem and Oinie* and *Smilin' Jack* situated characters there. The Senate's newsreel of Manila's fighting was described as the "most graphic to come out of the war." *Back to Bataan* gave the Philippine underground overdue recognition.

Events added attention. The Woman's Society of Christian Service of Camp Curtin Methodist Church, Sixth and Woodbine Streets, scheduled a speech on the islands. Lieutenant Carlos Romulo Jr. unveiled Japanese crimes and applauded Filipino partisans at the Penn Harris. Liberated Harrisburg missionaries arrived on the West Coast.

Disturbed Russian relations surfaced. Mark Sullivan's column expounded "troubled concern" about Soviet actions. The *Telegraph* believed the Russians would stand shoulder to shoulder. But a discussion at Beth El Temple billed "Wilson's Fourteen Points and the Big Three Agreement" made people wonder.

Nevertheless, Harrisburg retained affection for Russia. Russian War Relief held a *samovar* (an urn for heating water) tea. Executive Secretary Mrs. Earl Carter spoke of "An American Adventure on Spreading of Goods and Goodwill" before the Civic Club. At Russian War Relief headquarters, volunteers viewed *Diary of a Nazi*. Through its Red Cross program, the Quota Club contributed clothing.

A "poisoned" relationship agitated biracial ties. However, gestures beckoned at improvement. Churches heard from spokespeople. At the Forster Street YMCA, a Lincoln University professor "asked that every element of the population be integrated fully into the national stream of life in order that complete democracy be achieved." Kenneth Spencer, star of *Bataan* and *Cabin in the Sky*, performed solo at the Forum. State and Loew's showed *It Happened in Springfield*, a counter to "racial intolerance." The *Telegraph* praised its "intelligent, dramatic account of how one community has gone about the teaching of children in the ways of true democracy," adding the "plea is that we must learn to know and respect our neighbors, no matter what their race, creed or color is."

Noteworthy books appeared. Gunnar Myrdal's *An American Dilemma* attained regard as "a milestone in the history of American race relations." Works like Saunders Redding's *No Day of Triumph*, Lillian Smith's *Strange Fruit* and Richard Wright's *Black Boy* authored powerful narratives.

Wright's novel, reviewed by the Civic Club's Book Circle, generated tribute by Dorothy Canfield Fisher as "the chance to help bring to the thoughtful attention of intelligent, morally responsible Americans, the honest, dreadful, heart-breaking story of a Negro childhood and youth." The Beth El Temple's Dr. Magil examined Howard Fast's *Freedom Road*, a saga of post–Civil War Reconstruction conferring the dedication "to the men and women, black and white, yellow and brown, who had laid down their lives in the struggle against fascism."

Harrisburg proceeded against social disease. Cases went down in 1944. Authorities quarantined more detainees. They apprehended fewer Black prostitutes than white. More of the former carried infections.

The city's progress won laurels. In February, the Third Service Command's Colonel Wilfred A. Morgan credited Milliken and police "for excellent work performed in cooperation with the command in controlling venereal disease in this area." Later, Colonel Morgan again commended Harrisburg, expressing satisfaction "to know that my particular sub-district has reached this splendid high standard of efficiency in an attempt to preserve the good health of the Army."

Cinema exploited teen misbehavior. In January, the Rio's *Youth on Trial* scripted a woman judge hearing of her daughter's delinquency. It criticized parents for juvenile unruliness.

Society sought explanations. A Doris Blake reader blamed Karl Marx, surmising, "Owning to false teachings, communistic in spirit if not always in name, children are getting to feel they are superior to their parents."

State industrial output dropped. The city region recorded a 1 percent cut. Nevertheless, the WPB reported district projects amounted to $905 million by January.

Lieutenant General L.H. Campbell Jr., an army ordnance officer, lauded metal production. Campbell stated, "We are depending on the Harrisburg Steel Corporation for a lot of our shells and we are getting them." He appreciated their supply and dependability.

The internal threat loomed. The Senate's *This Is America* portrayed the FBI's exposing subversives and was called "one of the timeliest films to come this way." The Rio's *Jade Mask* had Charlie Chan helping Washington nullify the danger.

*On Guard* struck a response. Viewing its Nazi Bund encampments and New York rally, a female queried, "Was that here or in Germany?" A reviewer trusted movies "such as those might well be shown again and again if only to refresh the memories of the American public." John Ray Carlson

Shells manufactured by Harrisburg Steel. *Courtesy of the Historic Harrisburg Association.*

had edified in his publication: "*Under Cover* is not so much an exposé of the work of alien Nazi or Fascists agents as it is, ultimately, a warning to America of those factors which have led to the development of a nativist, nationalist, American Nazi or American Fascist movement which, like a spearhead, is poised to stab at Democracy."

The war came home. Movie houses ran *The Enemy Strikes*, a War Department documentary recounting the Bulge. Images of Germans filmed by a Nazi cameraman showed them "smoking American cigarets [*sic*] stolen from dead American soldiers."

Correspondent Ernie Pyle went to the Pacific. He wrote a *Telegraph* column. In January, Rabbi Magil examined his *Brave Men*, in which Pyle interviewed a Harrisburger, Captain Benjamin Halporn of 1500 State Street, on a vessel.

On April 18, a Japanese sniper killed Ernest Taylor Pyle on Ie Shima, a small island adjacent to Okinawa. A bereaving editorial solemnized, "TEARS FOR ERNIE."

Cinema feigned moods and emotions. *God Is My Co-Pilot* ranted at the Japanese. *A Guy, a Gal and a Pal* questioned defense labor's manliness. *Roughly Speaking* portrayed a family's sacrifice of three sons. Wait and worry issued from *Music for Millions* and *Thirty Seconds over Tokyo*. In the latter, Ted Lawson's wife reassures his acceptance after a leg amputation.

Movie tunes touched the grass roots. From *Here Come the WAVES*, "I Promise You" implied fidelity, and "There's a Fella Waitin' in Poughkeepsie" conjured soldiers' furlough. "Ac-Cent-Tchu-Ate the Positive," on *Your Hit Parade* for twelve weeks, became "the war's one great feel-good morale number."

The *Telegraph* ran comic relief. In January, Bob Hope's column "IT SAYS HERE" appeared. Hope performed on radio and did USO tours. His *I Never Left Home*, a travelogue of troop gigs, made the best-seller list. The comedian's movies counted *My Favorite Blonde*, *Road to Morocco*, *Star Spangled Rhythm*, *Let's Face It*, *They Got Me Covered* and *The Princess and the Pirate*.

At the Third Reich's twilight, Hollywood bared Nazi degeneracy. Loew's *Tomorrow the World* screened a professor's attempts to Americanize a German

German prisoners, runaways, recaptured by Carlisle police. *From the* Evening News. *Courtesy of PennLive.*

youth. An ad blurted, "Ja! I AM A NAZI WEREWOLF!" about "the terrifying story of a boy in America who turned out to be as cruel and dangerous as one of Hitler's henchmen."

Washington detailed fifteen thousand German prisoners locally, including in New Cumberland, Indiantown Gap and Middletown. Two employed at Carlisle ran off. At the Penn Harris, the Pennsylvania American Legion condemned their assignment to the Valley Forge General Hospital, resolving it "detrimental to the rehabilitation of the wounded American servicemen patients." An editorial asked, "Are We Coddling German Prisoners?" and inferred we might be.

In April, the German Zion Lutheran Church on Herr and Capital Streets deleted "German" from the name. Reverend William Lobsien said worship retained the language. He held that his congregation had no link to Germany. The title had checked the brethren's growth.

Der Harrisburg Maennerchor (translated "the Harrisburg Men's Choir"), the city's oldest male club, lost members. Established in 1867 to perpetuate the fatherland's legacy, the North Street fraternity deemphasized its German ties and remained open.

Reported Japanese atrocities saturated the press. In January, General MacArthur's liberation of prisoners revealed the extent. The *Evening News* carried Clark Lee's series in February and March, divulging tortures, starvations, batterings and murders. In April, a speaker recalled war crimes to pitch bonds.

The Rio reran *China Girl*, showing Japanese pilots maneuver "to strafe innocent Chinese civilians." The encore buttressed a conviction of mean-spirited carnage.

Nobe Frank corrected, tongue-in-cheek, a misapplication, writing that some "chemical company sends in a batch of ideas about rat extermination—not Japs—the four-legged plague spreaders." This as B-29s subjected Japan to incendiaries, called "Bacalls" in tribute to actress Lauren Bacall.

Der Harrisburg Maennerchor on North Street. *Photograph by Christine L.G. Ross.*

Some protested the callousness. When the American Legion in Oregon ordered Japanese Americans to dispossess and depart, the *Evening News* responded, "The splendid record of the Nisei fighters who have gone from our concentration camps into the Army might well serve to remind overzealous Americans that skin pigmentation in itself, is not a badge of disloyalty." A letter to the editor criticized Lee's characterization of Japanese as naturally inclined to "savage" behavior.

Given reports of atrocities in the Philippines, family members' freedom brought relief. Nurse Lieutenant Anna E. Williams, John Harris class of 1935, reached the West Coast. A Harrisburger heard his brother had been liberated at Manila's Santo Tomas University.

Many wartime relationships ended in divorce. In January, Dauphin County registered an upward trend. Still, before Easter, servicemen crowded the marriage office for licenses. Then nuptials dropped off. Breakups climbed.

Expectations of V-E Day ran high, but officials hoped to temper jubilance. They decided against a parade. Taverns, supported by the Dauphin County Clubs Association, would refrain from liquor sales. Milliken thought factory celebrations would allow work to resume. He proclaimed May 6 for worship to demonstrate "appreciation of spiritual guidance which we have received during these trying times."

*Left*: Lieutenant Anna E. Williams, John Harris High School graduate and former Harrisburg Hospital nurse, liberated from the Japanese. *From the* Evening News. *Courtesy of PennLive.*

*Right*: A marine and his wartime bride. *Author's collection.*

A Good Friday mood prevailed. Harrisburg readied for Easter. Industries, mainly steel, maintained operations. Traffic lessened from the previous year. Shoppers found markets out of hams. Scarcities dwindled turkeys and lamb. High point meats sold along with fish and eggs. Bountiful fruit, particularly bananas, carried high price tags. Plants and flowers lined counters.

The *Evening News* announced, "Germany's Easter parade will be strictly a Yank show." Worshipers, many military, thronged churches, asking for outcomes wistfully incanted on the front page:

> *Easter Prayer*
> *May it be a day of renewed promise*
> *That from this troubled world*
> *The cloud of war will be lifted,*
> *And all men live together,*
> *Free and unfettered.*
> *In tranquility and understanding.*

President Franklin D. Roosevelt. *Author's collection.*

President Roosevelt passed on April 12. His death stunned America. Extra press editions were released to convince doubters of terse radio reports.

President Harry S. Truman proclaimed a day of grieving. Harrisburg followed suit. Officials promoted the Seventh War Loan in FDR's name. At the Zembo Luncheon Club, members offered quiet prayer and lowered a flag. An editorial, "Franklin Delano Roosevelt," lamented that the republic "will long remember his service and his incredible record of breaking records."

Clergy conducted rites. Shaken and distressed, they promised to "unite with those who mourn this great loss in our country and throughout the world," elegizing that in the enshrinement of "his figure were crystalized the hopes of all liberty-loving peoples and those who face an unknown future in scarred and devastated lands across the seas."

The April 14 funeral stilled the city. Businesses halted temporarily except those war related. Groceries shut down for two hours. Some retailers and state liquor stores closed all day. Churches held services. Public institutions flew flags half-staff. Radio deleted entertainment. Stations broadcasted memorials, reverential compositions and news flashes. Movie houses stopped screenings at 6:00 p.m.

On April 18, Pocket Books published *Franklin Delano Roosevelt: A Memorial.* Written in a week and available to Harrisburgers, the encomium centered "the ideas he stood for and lived by, a record of devotion to freedom that made him great."

Harrisburg minded civil defense until May. School grounds held emergency medical facilities. The region serviced troop exercises by disaster units.

Once President Truman terminated the OCD programs, Milliken followed up. He returned state property, excluding "a hatchet and saw." When invoiced for both at three dollars, he exclaimed, "We paid the bill." The city surrendered medical supplies but sought fire-pumper purchases. From 1941, local defense outlays amounted to $69,785.

On May 7, Germany surrendered. The *Telegraph* broke the news. At Second and Walnut Streets, a newsstand sold out its copies. "V-E Day" blazed in a

Democracy banished totalitarianism. *From the* Harrisburg Telegraph. *Courtesy of PennLive.*

headline across the top of its front page. The *Evening News* bannered "END OF WAR SET FOR MIDNIGHT," caricaturing a pugilist knocking out Hitler after battering Mussolini and lampooning a frightened Japanese boxer and captioned "Next!"

Twenty-four hours later, the country celebrated. Mayor Milliken requested prayer. He mandated a noise restriction. Excepting a few shrilled whistles, citizens observed the ban.

The city discontinued a four-month brownout. Consequently, movie house signboards and storefront displays glistened.

Routine activities ceased. The Wednesday Club tabled a recital. Retailers, bars and liquor stores closed. After five years running, steel plants shut down. Flags flew at half-staff.

The YMCA held special observances. Looked on by armed forces personnel, attendants discarded a European map and hung a Pacific one on the foyer's wall.

Epigrams and symbols commercialized victory. Bowman's recited Lincoln's "and that government of the people, by the people, for the people, shall not perish from the earth" opposite a *Mein Kampf* image. Pomeroy's extolled "Let FREEDOM Ring," accompanied by the Liberty Bell and a row of United Nations banners. Sears Roebuck cheered "TRIUMPH…in the good American way," illustrated by a farmer driving a jeep, hauling milk cans in an idyllic and tranquil setting. Worth's eulogized "PEACE" with an angelic figure above the world, and Stroehmann Brothers pictured worshippers nodding thanks with a mother, a father and their daughter at church prayer.

On V-E Day, the WMC's local chief admonished employees to stay on the job. Hoping Germany's defeat would inspire until war's end, he credited workers for making V-E a reality.

Unlike November 11, 1918, Harrisburg greeted surrender with dignified sobriety. A calm reception welcomed capitulation. An absence of revelry and partying ruled. Residents prayed and attended church. Their demeanor acknowledged a devotion necessary to subdue Nippon.

9

# THE END

## May 1945–September 1945

Europe enjoyed peace, but Pacific combat raged. In May, the War Department reported over forty-three thousand air force casualties. The army and navy recorded nearly one million lost. Thousands died weekly.

Casualties hit home. Emma Foster, a nurse serving the Flying Tigers in China, lost her husband, John E. Petach. Actor Dane Clark impersonated Petach in *God Is My Co-Pilot*. The family of a city sailor killed on the USS *Franklin* examined the displayed aircraft carrier's debris.

Conscription counteracted losses. The draft board drummed calls throughout the spring and summer.

Recruiting intensified. The military needed radar trainees. Marines took seventeen-year-olds. Sears recognized the WACs' three-year service, and Harrisburg sponsored an anniversary parade. The Loew's *Keep Your Powder Dry*, a recruitment pitch, starred "Lana Turner, Laraine Day, and Susan Peters as WACs."

The navy wanted WAVES to free men for the Pacific. In June, recruiters searched for 150 volunteers. WAVES paraded. They gave a dinner at their Harrisburg Academy headquarters. A full-page ad toasted, "Well done, WAVES!" and urged "Join the WAVES Now!"

Officials relaxed wartime procedures. Mayor Milliken permitted blackout curtain removal. Effective June 30, he shut down the Harrisburg–Dauphin County Defense Council. Its victory gardens continued under the park's office. The Disaster Committee absorbed its Salvage Committee.

Well-drilled WAVES march down Second Street in the D-Day anniversary parade. *From the* Evening News. *Courtesy of PennLive.*

The Locust Street Servicemen's Center maintained operation. Surplus Red Cross stocks reverted back to the agency. Harrisburg Flotilla 53, a river defense unit, went off duty.

Observances merged patriotism and spirituality. Churches remembered Mother's Day. Radio linked victory to the celebration, as did a Forum program by Catholic High. The same venue scheduled the eighteenth annual Community Mother's Day commemorative, illuminated by the "Spiritual Victory for the Mothers of America." The First Baptist Church's Reverend Charles Reid Leech emphasized "the alliance of education and religion as the only means of saving our Country from the fate that has come to Germany."

Harrisburg went all out for Memorial Day. Officials invited veterans, scouts, pupils and military personnel to parade and asked residents to fly flags along the march. Rotaries heard a clergyman talk of warfare's dissipation, and schools presented special performances. Columnist Nobe Frank recalled

Poppy Day as the holiday's old name, a First World War retrospective. The *Evening News* memorialized, "Humbly we bow in memory of heroes and deed" and invoked, "It is rather for us to be here dedicated to the great task remaining before us."

Groups rallied for Flag Day. The Sons of the American Revolution, Harris Ferry chapter, welcomed a Forum audience. The Brotherhood of Temple Beth El planned dancing. The Elks held rites at Reservoir Park. Also there, the commander of the municipal sub-district in the Third Service Command glorified the emblem that "has never entered battle save in the cause of human liberty." The former grand chaplain of Unity Lodge 71, Colored Elks, revealed the "Contribution to the Flag by the American Negro" at North Sixth Street.

A citizen complained of disregard for the standard. Writing to the *Evening News*, the correspondent gave advice on etiquette during the national anthem. To the writer's chagrin, individuals of a mosque audience reversed chair seats, moved about and exited while singers rendered.

Comfortable weather and wartime restrictions greeted Harrisburg on the Fourth. Temperatures registered under average and reached mid-eighty by noon. Thousands gathered in parks, but defense industries and military installations functioned. Transportation experienced no exceptional business. Bans prohibited "firecrackers, Roman candles, skyrockets, spinning wheels."

Symbolic of the day, the *Evening News*'s front page featured marching revolutionary soldiers followed by a flag and marines raising the banner on Iwo Jima.

In August, the Sunday movies dispute resurfaced. Theaters distributed forms for patrons' signatures. Enough endorsements would petition the question the next election.

The *Evening News* viewed Sabbath cinema as "ANOTHER THREAT," claiming wholesome movies shown to soldiers made Sunday films unnecessary and adding, "What the good people of this community must determine is whether Harrisburg's Sabbath is such a pointless, meaningless day that its spiritual importance can be ignored." Regardless, moviegoers satisfied a petition. A vote would decide the issue.

V-E Day reduced the demand for blood. The Front and South Streets center ended service. Before closing on May 18, it posted donors and scheduled "banner donation days." Two days before, few volunteers came. But the next day, 31 joined the Gallon Club, and 141 gave. Roy Dively of Sayford Street contributed a seventieth time. The last day, 300 donors appeared. Later, a tea attended its closure.

By mid-May, the center procured 173,873 blood gifts—47,040 donated at Front Street and 126,833 via mobiles. Harrisburg's unit, "smallest of 35 centers in the Country, had the best record of any on a per capita basis during its two and one-half years of operation." The army's surgeon general applauded the contribution.

The Red Cross fulfilled duties and sought assistance. It kept prisoners' families informed and produced sweaters. The agency needed help. Appeals went out for hospital aides. An ad pleaded, "THE RED CROSS NEEDS YOUR SERVICE." An editorial called recruitment for medical facilities an "immediate and urgent task" and reminded residents that the demand persisted. School pupils and Boys' Club members participated. The *Evening News* editorialized "FAR FROM ENDED," and since "Japan continues to fight," one hopes "the shrinkage in collection does not mean a corresponding shrinkage in home front cooperation in winning the war."

From the Pacific, Admiral Chester W. Nimitz notified the state of the necessity of paper conservation. Speaking before the Optimists, salvage committee executive secretary Colley S. Baker deplored the loss of paper in Harrisburg's incinerators. Meanwhile, the comic strip *Nancy* restated the preservative need.

Newspapers sacrificed. In June, complying with Washington's regulations, the *Evening News* cut funnys space and initiated more restrictions. The *Telegraph* eliminated twelve ad lines "in order to give our readers full and complete news coverage as well as our regular features and comics."

With youngsters' aid, officials assembled cans on August 4. Four months had passed since the last roundup. Harrisburg assumed a high tonnage. The day before, Pomeroy's reminded residents of tin's uses and of Japan's source domination. Its ad asked householders to be a "Tin Soldier" and pointed out, "America's only 'tin mines' are in your kitchen!" For pickup, it instructed, make "sure all tin cans are properly processed and placed on the curb in front of your home."

The total disappointed. Gatherers amassed sixty tons. Officials judged the effort "fair" but, given tin's shortage, wished for more.

Harrisburg tended victory gardens. Dr. Ross advised on transplants and crops. (He favored lima beans.) A Nineteenth and Swatara Streets store marketed "plater laths," convenient for staking tomatoes and poling beans. Ross devised military metaphors like "invasion," "general," "Scouting" and "defense" to outfox insects. Japanese beetles raided in June. In August, the Dobbin's Duster arrived, analogous to the unforeseen atomic bomb, a powder disperser for battling bugs.

Private business prepared for peace. Dodge-Plymouth salesmen met to examine sales and services. W.M. Hollinger purchased seventeen acres, a sometime dump. It encompassed Twenty-First, Twenty-Fourth, Berryhill and Swatara Streets, and Hollinger leveled the tract for two hundred homes, awaiting supplies and labor.

July brought contractors good news. The National Housing Agency freed materials for 225 units. The release imposed no occupancy limits. Officials conceded that a dwelling shortfall harmed wartime progress and "hoped that builders will give preference to local industries engaged in war production and military establishments, evictees, returning veterans and servicemen's families."

Curbs lingered. State police wanted Harrisburg's help to deter speeding. Lectured motorists learned that Germany's defeat failed to excuse acceleration's wears on tires. The vehicle and rubber economy disallowed buses for the Farm Show's circus. The ODT prohibited busing for Reservoir Park's Romper Day. The city postponed Kipona.

Uncollected ashes and unclean surroundings blighted Harrisburg. Striking ash men delayed pickups. Milliken contemplated employing German prisoners. Industries generated filth. Smoke irritated. A letter to the *Evening News* deplored the "dirty streets, sidewalks and general dowdiness of the city." The paper remembered that Harrisburg "once had a reputation for tidiness and efficient municipal government."

Notwithstanding V-E Day, schools pursued war-inspired activities. The district continued defense courses such as "radio, auto-mechanic, and welding" at Harris and Penn, despite withdrawal of federal moneys. Penn's band performed patriotic numbers. A Harris Youth Forum debated "Should Congress Enact a Law to Provide for Compulsory Military Training?"

Graduation exercises entertained duration's themes. Camp Curtin revived "I Am an American." William Penn's thirty-fifth commencement spotlighted conflict deterrence through educating anew the peoples of Axis countries. The program likewise congratulated schools for classes preparing women as defense workers. Catholic High emphasized loyalty.

In the summer, youth stayed engaged. Fourth Street's Drama Club performed for Red Cross funds. The show, staged between two houses by a garage, netted over twenty-eight dollars.

Juvenile crime brought a concern for kids. Accompanied by U.S. banners at Reservoir Park, Harrisburg's Civic Club awarded thirty-five children for upright conduct on playgrounds.

More motoring and bicycling accented road safety. In response, the Keystone Automobile Club formulated regulations to reduce mishaps.

The new school year neared. Administrators asked employed youth to return. The district planned no program changes.

The armed forces still recruited dogs. One came back. City council hedged acceptance of Blue, a former police dog. The animal knew "vicious tricks" and could resist pet demeanor. Officials thought of disposal. Fortunately, the Pacific returnee found comfort at the Harrisburg Military Post on Fifteenth Street and the By-Pass.

In August, residents learned of a veteran's sorrow. After homecoming, he realized someone had abducted Belle, his hunting hound. The *Evening News* qualified the thief as a "claimant for the dubious title of 'meanest man in Harrisburg.'"

On May 14, the city kicked off the Seventh War Loan. Among much fanfare, officials aimed to raise $5.9 million on "B-Day." Hoop-la styled bond marketing.

Programs pushed the campaign. Downtown theaters bustled the short film *All-Star Bond Rally*. Henry I. Marshall's "It's the Seventh" played on the radio and appeared in the *Evening News*. The paper wanted residents to save the song "and Play It on Your Piano! Keep it as a souvenir of the mighty 7th War Loan." Its lyrics alluded to fortitude and retribution:

*It's the 7th—the lucky 7th*
*And we'll all put it over with a cheer*
*And for every Iwo hero*
*We'll down another zero*
*We don't forget Pearl Harbor never fear*
*We stand up in the 7th at the ball game*
*We won't sit down at all-in the Bond game*
*It's the 7th—the lucky 7th*
*Let's go while the victory is near.*

Targeting above the previous loan, a military concert and star Claude Rains's appearance opened the campaign. The next day, Rains showed up at the Rio before store employees paraded, a march led by Harris's band. The *Evening News* headlined "Buy War Bonds Today and Keep Them."

The army and navy went all out. Pilots exhibited aircraft. They offered rides for bonds. Fighters overflew the city. Infantry mocked an assault on an imaginary stronghold at the island. Moreover, purchasers gained admission to baseball between Middletown's Technical Service Command and the America League's Philadelphia Athletics. The Marine Corps Women's Reserve Band, on an eastern tour, entertained at the Forum. The Dauphin County War Finance Committee sponsored *Calliope Capers*, a soldiers' comedy attended by actors Adolph Menjou, Ralph Bellamy, Ruth Hussay and Frances Dee.

Harrisburg declared "Peggy Ann Garner Day." A parade and a city hall ceremony hailed the child star. Garner, cast in *A Tree Grows in Brooklyn*, took part in the Forum's *A Cavalcade of Youth*, a local talent showcase.

To back the drive, the *Evening News* conceived limerick competitions, running for three weeks with victors awarded fifty-dollar bonds. Entrants pilloried the Japanese:

> *The fight for Japan's just begun*
> *Let's keep the Nips on the run*
> *Buy bonds one and all*
> *Hasten Tokyo's fall*
> —*May 24* [accompanied by a cartoon image of a fleeing Japanese person]

> *Our Air Force is being augmented*
> *To fight Japs who are more than demented*
> *But to buy planes and man ships*
> *Takes a huge bag of chips*
> *BUY BONDS TIL THOSE SKUNKS ARE DE-SCENTED*
> —*May 29*

> *Let's make short work of the Jap*
> *Brush him off the face of the map*
> *Buy bonds all the while*
> *Beat them back to their isle*
> *PUT CHEESE IN THE NIPPONESE TRAP*
> —*June 2*

Ethel M. Buffington, an Edison English instructor and General Dwight D. Eisenhower's cousin, invoked muster and sacrifice:

> *Let's rally, my friends, to the call*
> *Buy bonds and more bonds one and all*

*Dig down in your jeans*
*Come across with the beans*
*AND THE AX ON THE AXIS WILL FALL*
*—May 28*

One winner yearned for her lover:

*Thank your stars you've got the dough*
*To blast the Japs from Tokyo*
*So quick as a flash*
*Let's take all our cash*
*HELP BRING ME BACK "MY ROMEO"*
*—May 31*

Comic strips framed the push. *Donald Duck* plastered "Mighty 7th War Loan" on a brick building. In turn, *Thimble Theater*, *The Nebbs*, *Bringing Up Father* and *Little Annie Rooney* rallied.

Businesses heralded bonds. For a purchase, Bowman's offered a pamphlet describing the war's battles. The D and H Distributing Company donated a Thor Electric Ironer to the Dauphin County War Finance Committee. The Gold-Tone Studios engaged in a competition by *Parents* magazine. Families entered babies, and bonds went for prizes. Also, Morris Square Deal Jewelers awarded the same to victors in a When Will the War End challenge.

Retailers used sketches and emblems. The Peanut Store pictured a naval gun crew. The A and P displayed the *V*, accompanied by the Iwo flag raising.

Ordinary people mobilized. Four hundred women volunteered, and Penn students bought bonds. Harris girls created an honor roll of service personnel for whom buyers secured bonds. Shimmel's pupils and staff sold over $9,000 worth.

Organizations joined the effort. The Y's Men's Club announced sales. The Charity S. Martin Chapter of the WIVES, the Harrisburg unit of the National Organization of Wives of Servicemen, prepared a quota. The Bolton Hotel's entertainers interrupted a performance to peddle bonds. Legionnaires and Rotarians took part.

Press reports measured progress. Chairman Ben Wolfe despaired about reaching the goal. But by mid-July, Harrisburg and Dauphin County exceeded projections.

Despite discord, Harrisburg appreciated Russia. The Senate ran *The People's Avenger*. The Colonial billed *Counter-Attack*, a film that "can re-establish in the minds of doubting Americans just what Russia did do in turning the tide of the war." For readers, Mrs. Russell Melchoir reviewed William L. White's *Report on the Russians* and Edmund Stevens's *Russia Is No Riddle* at the Civic Club's Book Circle. The Russian War Relief Society produced clothing and, as the newly named American Society of Russian Relief, maintained aid to the Soviets. One of the country's dishes came recommended. Goloubtzy, a rice mix, stretched meat.

Philippine liberations magnified affiliation. A missionary, visiting his Harrisburg brother, credited General MacArthur with his salvation. In May, the Episcopal Church planned missions. The Rio reran *So Proudly We Hail*, judged "one of the ten best pictures of 1943," coinciding with Lieutenant Williams's return. During a landing craft display, the naval depot chief conversed with a Bataan survivor. In August, the Pennsylvania Guard's First Cavalry devoted its Horse Show to Corregidor defender Lieutenant General Jonathan Wainwright. Adele, his wife, arrived and reminisced on her city residence and education. Before the war, the Wainwrights stopped by frequently.

The OPA kept a vigil. The *Telegraph* published "OPA Notes," "Ration Reminders" and price tables. Regulations carried over. Black markets sullied motor fuel and foods. *Barnaby* shamed Harrisburgers for violations. Court actions ensued.

Shortages persisted. Slaughterhouses received supervision. Sugar curbs undersupplied the Harrisburg Coca-Cola Bottling Works, but executives promised to retain the "quality of our drink and to maintain an equitable distribution system to serve all our customers equally and that we will do." A *Cap Stubbs and Tippie* character sighed that sufficient points might not consummate a sugar purchase.

Price control showed no letup. Ceilings capped fruit and vegetables. Eggs required lids. Used refrigerators came under sales rules. Scrutiny oversaw rents and car repairs. When soldiers protested a dollar charge for shoeshines, Young ordered an investigation.

The OPA directed stores to post charges. In July, it circulated pamphlets through retailers and associations, convinced "such methods of price checking a powerful weapon to help smash black market sales."

Prosecutions followed violations. Agents urged penalties for excessive beer prices by Acri and Fisher and for above-ceiling sales by the Harrisburg Waste Paper Company. The office fined Clasters for over-capping watches. The Maple Grove Café paid $200 for exceeding. In June, the OPA initiated fourteen cases. At the outset of August, it indicted Mary Lalos Shoe Repairs on Market Street, Warner Motors and Walton Radiator Works on South Cameron, Fisher-Bell Motor Company on Sassatras and Lee Brothers on North Third. Additional suits occurred later.

Now and then, maximums came down or off. Strawberries underwent reduction. Blessed with large outputs, the agency eliminated ceilings "from snap beans, cucumbers, sweet peppers and eggplant."

Still concerned about prices and infractions, Young begged volunteers to stay. With gas rationing lifted, crooks might target meat, fat and butter. Despite some cases, the OPA asserted black marketing "never got a foot hold here," and the office "held the price line against inflation."

Stamp usage confused. A child heard her grandparent refer to a soldier's points short for service release. She reacted, "Grandmother…you have a lot of red and blue points. Why don't you send him enough so he can come home?"

Foodstuffs abuse annoyed people. Given the food shortage, a shop owner stopped bean and pea sales for blowguns. The State's *Christmas in Connecticut* offended for its vivid and tempting spread "of conspicuous consumption," giving an unfavorable picture of the homefront.

In June, the Senate screened *Something You Didn't Eat*, a Disney cartoon making "a plea for consumption of the basic seven food groups to insure [*sic*] public health."

Harrisburg greeted the touring Evelyn Keyes. Milliken presented the actress with a municipal key before an Exchange Club appearance. Her agenda included visits to Indiantown Gap and Middletown medical centers.

Those abroad were remembered. Pomeroy's free booklet for families, mailed uncharged, of sixty-four pages fit a pocket and reprinted "Post Yarns" (the *Saturday Evening Post* selections). For those deployed in the Philippines, a bit of Capitol Park soil departed. Once there, it montaged as U.S. ground. The pile, labeled Homesick Hill, enabled sailors to tramp native land.

Harrisburg attended returnees. A county Returned Veteran's Information and Referral Center advised on jobs and other matters, the beneficiary of a municipal donation. The Veterans' Financial Advisory Service aided GI Bill lending. A Veteran Advisory Committee offered assistance. Returnees received guidance concerning life insurance.

Former servicemen wanted startups. The OPA's District Veterans' Relations Advisory Committee helped. Incorporated confectionary got extra sugar. The Smaller War Plants Corporation obliged the purchase of commercial vehicles.

Work became the priority. Over one hundred veterans found jobs in the four weeks preceding May 21. Harrisburg gave preference for its offices.

Actress Evelyn Keyes, in Harrisburg to entertain the troops and a guest of the Exchange Club, receives the key to the city. *From the* Evening News. *Courtesy of PennLive.*

Pointing to the significance of this work, *Lem and Oinie* pictured returnees pursuing employment.

Support groups began. At the YMCA, veterans founded the Harrisburg Post, No. 1, AMVETS, for the honorably discharged and inaugurated a membership campaign. The city provided meeting rooms. In July, former prisoners of the Germans planned the Gerfanogaidiers Club, with over one hundred eligible. The new Next of Kin of Prisoners of War made arrangements to embrace POWs.

The adjustment to civilian life raised questions. Harrisburg State Hospital director Dr. Howard K. Petry believed that "the returning veteran will be no problem." Petry discredited a sympathetic sorrow. Rather, he said, the returnee needs loyal companions and a spouse as well as a boss willing to employ.

By June, movies trended away from war and scripted veterans' tales. The Rio's *The Man Who Walked Alone* described returnee difficulties. *Tomorrow Is Here*, a "forthcoming production," would story veterans released from medical facilities. In September, the Colonial's *Pride of the Marines* portrayed a blinded Guadalcanal hero's struggle.

Scams beset military families. The commander of the Third Service Command's Harrisburg subdivision warned of con artists promising to name the killed and missing in a fictitious Hall of Fame. Schemers likewise proposed a "Heroes Memorial Book."

A movie critic liked the Senate's revival of *Imitation of Life*. Arriving during race agitation, it had been panned for "the old stereotype of contended Mammy, and the tragic mulatto; and the ancient ideas about the mixture of the races." But the *Telegraph* saw a public service by Hollywood "trying to cement the relationship of all the people of this country, and other countries as well."

War's conclusion had the paper ponder Hollywood's future and applaud its yesterday. One prospective would recite "the evil deeds and ideals of the European warlords." Such fare would accentuate World War II's price. Films had aided the nation with news and amusement. Many cited the Pacific, dramatizing suffering and sacrifice. The paper noted their drop-off and a turn to the returnees.

The *Film Daily Yearbook of Motion Pictures* estimated moviegoing. Each week in 1944, ninety-five million attended, ten million above 1941. A theater existed for every eight thousand individuals and a seat per twelve residents.

Documentaries became common. Downtown cinema exhibited *The Battle of San Pietro*, billed as "no finer tribute to the foot soldier," and *To the Shores of Iwo Jima*, in which marine cameramen died. *Target Tokyo* featured raiding B-29s. The navy chronicled *Battle of Supply* and *The Fleet That Came to Stay*. *Policing Germany* narrated a Nazi town's rehabilitation under the Allies.

In May, the *Evening News* announced *Wilson*'s revival. Professor James T. Shotwell composed a biography as a study guide. The *Telegraph* called the film a must-see and believed it "will be a strong force in promoting an enduring peace." *Wilson* reappeared at the State in August and gathered accolades for espousing internationalism.

In July, the *Telegraph*'s film column detected less warfare and more escapism. Considering labor and material shortages, audiences could expect revivals.

Crime busied law enforcement and public hygiene. Two Harrisburgers pled culpable for construction store thievery in Mechanicsburg. The Rio's *Youth Aflame* reverberated teen wrongdoing, plugged, "What's Wrong with Modern Youth?" and "A DARING EXPOSE OF JUVENILE DELINQUENCY." Police went after streetwalkers. Awarded for combating contagion, health officials joined police agencies, state officials, military agents, Community Chest officers and Travelers Aid to "further the current campaign to stamp out venereal diseases, especially among those of the armed services."

City streets were hazards. Fights hurt three seamen in June. The next month, a brawl at Third and Herr Streets drew hundreds. In August, a sailor knifed a woman in a scrap at Monroe and Cumberland. The same month, police jailed thieves, a woman and Mexicans among them.

German prisoners absconded. In June, four fled the New Cumberland Reception Center, spending twelve hours on the run. A POW working at a Lebanon macaroni plant disappeared. In August, two more bolted, one from Indiantown Gap and the other from Middletown Air Depot. A boy recaptured the latter. One escapee from Lineboro, Maryland, had Harrisburg's FBI on his tail. Authorities caught a Gap runaway south of the Mason-Dixon line.

As newspapers reported fleeing Germans, the Colonial booked *Escape in the Desert*, portraying Nazi fugitives and their hostages holed up in an Arizona motel.

Media belittlement of the Japanese continued uninterrupted. The editorial "SUICIDAL STUPIDITY" asserted, "The Jap is not only inhuman, he is also inefficient." *Joe Palooka* referred to a cruel Nipponese serpent. A woman in *Scorchy Smith* alluded to "the yellow ones." *Smilin' Jack* satirized facial expressions. Screenplays storied Japan's lack of international ethics. The Loew's *Blood on the Sun* detailed Tokyo's expansionist schemes. The Senate's *Betrayal from the East* exposed "fairly, graphic scenes of Japanese torture" and "Nip treachery in the U.S." prior to December 7.

In August, the United States dropped atomic bombs on Japan. With a double-sized, front-page headline "HIROSHIMA IN RUINS," the *Telegraph* echoed Samuel F.B. Morse's, "What Hath God Wrought?" The *Evening News* prophesied, "There won't be much left after that next war." Once a second bomb devastated Nagasaki, the paper punned, "The nearsighted Jap must be seeing scrapheap," followed by "Taps seem to be near for the Japs." The *Telegraph* snarled, "Surrender or Perish."

The city pondered a new era. Would a third conflict be bearable? Furthermore, what action would the United States take to control the bomb?

On August 10, a triple-sized headline blared, "JAPAN SUBMITS SURRENDER PLEA." Celebrating would close liquor stores and bars. Retailers planned time off for employees. A two-hour parade of two sections would converge on State Street and pass before a reviewing platform.

On August 15, newspapers heralded, "JAP CAPITULATION SPEEDED," "WORLD TURNS TO PEACE" and "STIFF TERMS FOR JAPAN." Harrisburg rejoiced.

After a calm August 14, the city let loose. Celebrants crowded avenues. Employers released workers. Noisemakers split ears. Paper and confetti blanketed Market Square. Patrons dashed from hotel restaurants, taverns,

V-J Day celebrated on Market Square. *From* the Evening News. *Courtesy of PennLive.*

cafés, bars and theaters. Women heading for a USO changed direction to dance in the streets. Crowds halted vehicles. Buses stopped their runs. At Third and Market Streets, patrolman Charles Ross "said that people were breaking every rule in the book," yet he appeared unfazed. On Fourth and Market, officer Earl Wallet, realizing the racket muffled his whistle, resorted to a night stick to direct traffic. Automobiles cruised, blazing American flags.

As residents flocked downtown, baseball games ended in mid-innings. Players darted from one field while teammates batted and outs accumulated. A player, advancing to home base, snatched his coat, kept running and headed out. Despite a fourth-inning tie at Twenty-First and Berryhill Streets, when loudspeakers broadcasted Japan's surrender, spectators made merry, and umpire Chubby Fry called the game.

Military police glanced away while the uniformed frolicked. Gyrenes kissed female bystanders, living up to "marines had the situation well in hand." Soldiers carting liquor invited onlookers to imbibe. A seaman, hauling another by his side, scampered down an alley.

In spite of the "reckless abandon," revelry caused no problems. Jostling and bumping occurred but without fistfights and property damage.

Clergy slated services. Rites held in the Forum attracted thousands. Residents came to Reservoir Park, Capitol Park and Zembo Mosque. Churches ministered beyond the two-day celebration.

WAVES parade to celebrate victory. *From the* Evening News. *Courtesy of PennLive.*

Biblical symbolism exalted V-J. Day. The *Telegraph* acknowledged God and solicited His might: "This is the day of Freedom's crowning hour; this day the powers of darkness took flight; this day the sun broke over a world at peace for the first time in 14 years. It is a good, a blessed day, a day to render thanks and beseech Almighty strength to carry on the burdens of peace won at a frightful price."

Ads mentioned victory's indebtedness. Schell's Seed Store, Worth's and Hoover's credited divine intervention and supplication. Pomeroy's and Stark Brothers applauded freedom's perpetuation. H.L. Green spelled out its cost: "The battle has been long: the heartbreak sad: the losses many." Moreover, Pomeroy's blessed the armed forces, saying, "We go to live together in that peace so long sought after." Klevan Brothers resurrected George M. Cohan's "IT'S OVER OVER THERE."

Normality returned by August 17. Grocers and druggists resumed business. Liquor and beer outlets reopened. Filling stations reported runs on non-rationed gas. Motorists took to the roads, ignoring V.D. Leisure's tire warning.

Japan's surrender permitted Williams Grove races. Speedway officials received assent and advertised restart.

V-J Day slowed industry. By August 16, metal plants had shut down. Harrisburg Steel lost contracts, discharged employees and initiated reconversions. The PRR dismissed laborers, including Mexicans. The USES announced an unemployment jump, mostly from steel.

Harrisburg claimed a role for Axis defeat, earning a hub distinction and pride as a "beehive of industry." Women labored in steel mills. Railroads moved goods. Corporations won recognition. For assisting, PPL accepted the 1944 Laura McCall Award for its "home service departments in the wartime program of food conservation and preservation and in emphasizing the care, maintenance and use of electrical equipment in the home."

Green thumbs did their part, tilling twelve thousand victory gardens on city-leased land and cultivating $765,000 in fruits and vegetables. The statistics excepted private home plots.

Victory came with a price—539 area service personnel died. Two families sacrificed 2 sons. Over 7,000 attended a September 1, 1946 commemorative at Reservoir Park for those lost.

On August 9, 1999, the *Patriot-News* published under "Stories of the Century" the following: "In January 1943, Cecelia W. Jarvins of Walnut Street, Harrisburg, became the first black woman to join the Women's Army Corps. A nurse, she entered the medical branch. She died in April 1996 at 96."

# BIBLIOGRAPHY

## *Books*


Basinger, Jeanine. *The World War II Combat Film: Anatomy of a Genre.* New York: Columbia University Press, 1986.

Bogle, Donald. *Toms, Coons, Mulattoes, Mammies, and Bucks: An Interpretive History of Blacks in American Films.* New York: Bantam Books, 1973.

Braverman, Jordan. *To Hasten the Homecoming: How Americans Fought World War II Through the Media.* Lanham, MD: Rowman and Littlefield, 2015.

Carlson, John Roy. *Under Cover: My Four Years in the Nazi Underworld of America—The Amazing Revelation of How Axis Agents and Our Enemies Within Are Now Plotting to Destroy the United States.* New York: E.P. Dutton and Co., 1943.

Clark, Walter Van Tilburg. *The Ox-Bow Incident.* New York: New American Library, 1960.

Donald, Ralph. *Hollywood Enlists! Propaganda Films of World War II.* Lanham, MD: Rowman and Littlefield, 2017.

Erenberg, Lewis A., and Susan E. Hirsch, eds. *The War in American Culture: Society and Consciousness During World War II.* Chicago: University of Chicago Press, 1996.

Fast, Howard. *Freedom Road.* New York: Bantam Books, 1979.

Foertsch, Jacqueline. *American Culture in the 1940s.* Edinburgh: Edinburgh University Press, 2008.

Friend, Theodore. *The Blue-Eyed Enemy: Japan Against the West in Java and Luzon, 1942–1945.* Princeton, NJ: Princeton University Press, 1988.

Geddes, Donald Porter, ed. *Franklin Delano Roosevelt: A Memorial.* New York: Pocket Books, 1945.

Goodman, Jack, ed. *While You Were Gone: A Report on Wartime Life in the United States.* New York: Da Capo Press, 1974.

Harmon, Lieutenant Tom. *Pilots Also Pray.* New York: Thomas Y. Crowell Company, 1944.

Jones, John Bush. *The Songs That Fought the War: Popular Music and the Home Front, 1939–1945.* Waltham, MA: Brandeis University Press, 2006.

Klein, Maury. *A Call to Arms: Mobilizing America for World War II.* New York: Bloomsbury Press, 2013.

Koppes, Clayton R., and Gregory D. Black. *Hollywood Goes to War: How Politics, Profits, and Propaganda Shaped World War II Movies*. New York: Free Press, 1987.

Lawson, Captain Ted W. *Thirty Seconds over Tokyo*. Edited by Robert Considine. New York: Random House, 1943.

Lingeman, Richard R. *Don't You Know There's a War On? The American Home Front, 1941–1945*. New York: G.P. Putnam's Sons, 1970.

Maynard, Richard A. *The Black Man on Film: Racial Stereotyping*. Rochelle Park, NJ: Hayden Book Company, 1974.

McCoy, Commander Melvyn H., USN, and Lieutenant Colonel S.M. Mellnik, USA. *Ten Escape from Tojo*. As told to Lieutenant Welbourn Kelley, USNR. New York: Farrar and Rinehard, 1944.

McLaughlin, Robert L., and Sally E. Parry. *We'll Always Have the Movies: American Cinema During World War II*. Lexington: University Press of Kentucky, 2006.

Norman, Elizabeth M. *We Band of Angels: The Untold Story of American Nurses Trapped on Bataan by the Japanese*. New York: Random House, 1999.

Parrish, Thomas, and Brigadier General S.L.A. Marshall, eds. *The Simon and Schuster Encyclopedia of World War II*. New York: Simon and Schuster, 1978.

Perrett, Geoffrey. *Days of Sadness, Years of Triumph: The American People 1939–1945*. Baltimore, MD: Penguin Books, 1973.

Perry, Richard J. *United We Stand!: A Visual Journey of Wartime Patriotism*. Portland, OR: Collectors Press, 2002.

Preston, Andrew. *Sword of the Spirit, Shield of Faith: Religion in American War and Diplomacy*. New York: Alfred A. Knopf, 2012.

Pyle, Ernie. *Brave Men*. New York: Henry Holt, 1944.

———. *Here Is Your War*. New York: Pocket Books, 1944.

Romulo, Colonel Carlos P. *I Saw the Fall of the Philippines*. Garden City, NY: Doubleday, Doran and Company, 1943.

Rose, Kenneth D. *Myth and the Greatest Generation: A Social History of Americans in World War II*. New York: Routledge, 2012.

Rottman, Gordon L. *Fubar: Soldier Slang of World War II*. New York: Chartwell Books, 2017.

Scott, Colonel Robert L. *God Is My Co-Pilot*. New York: Ballantine Books, 1957.

Seagrave, Gordon S. *Burma Surgeon*. New York: W.W. Norton, 1943.

Shull, Michael S., and David Edward Wilt, eds. *Hollywood War Films, 1937–1945: An Exhaustive Filmography of American Feature-Length Motion Pictures Relating to World War II*. Jefferson, NC: McFarland and Company, 1996.

Slotkin, Richard. *Gunfighter Nation: The Myth of the Frontier in Twentieth-Century America*. New York: Harper Perennial, 1993.

Steinbeck, John. *The Moon Is Down*. New York: Viking, 1942.

Taylor, Jackson. *The Blue Orchard*. New York: Simon and Schuster, 2010.

Tregaskis, Richard. *Guadalcanal Diary*. New York: Random House, 1943.

Westbrook, Robert B. *Why We Fought: Forging American Obligations in World War II*. Washington, D.C.: Smithsonian Books, 2004.

Williams, Major Al. *Airpower*. New York: Coward-McCann, 1940.

Winchell, Meghan K. *Good Girls, Good Food, Good Fun: The Story of USO Hostesses During World War II*. Chapel Hill: University of North Carolina Press, 2008.

Wright, Richard. *Black Boy: A Record of Childhood and Youth*. New York: Harper and Row, 1966.
Ziff, William B. *The Gentlemen Talk of Peace*. New York: Macmillan, 1944.

## *Newspapers*

*Evening News*, December 6, 1941–September 3, 1945.
*Harrisburg Sunday Courier*, December 7, 1941–September 27, 1942.
*Harrisburg Telegraph*, December 7, 1941–September 5, 1945.
*Patriot-News*, December 8, 1941, August 9, 1999.

## *Articles*

Auel, Lisa B. "Buddies: Soldiers and Animals in World War II." *Prologue* 28 (Fall 1996): 232–8.
Guglielmo, Thomas A. "A Martial Freedom Movement: Black G.I.s' Political Struggles during World War II." *Journal of American History* 104 (2018): 879–903.
Ross, Rodney J. "The Filipino Reaction to a Celluloid Insult: President Manuel Quezon Censures *The Real Glory*." *Pilipinas* 23 (Fall 1994): 61–72.
Zubovich, Gene. "For Human Rights Abroad, against Jim Crow at Home: The Political Mobilization of American Ecumenical Protestants in the World War II Era." *Journal of American History* 105 (2018): 267–90.

## *Miscellaneous*

"Glenn Miller and His Orchestra." Record album jacket. New York: Twentieth Fox Record Corporation, TCF-100–2.
Washington National Records Center, Record Group 44, Box 1842, entry 144, Suitland, MD. OWI Field representative report from Pennsylvania.
Witmer, Lois. "Memories of Pomeroy's." Dauphin County Library. Unpublished.

## *Internet*

Fertenbaugh, Jen. "History and Community: Der Harrisburg Maennerchor Marks 150 Years of Fraternity, Service." *The Burg*, December 29, 2017. https://theburgnews.com.
Hardison, Lizzy. "My City Was Gone: How Redlining Helped Segregate, Blight Harrisburg." *The Burg*, August 31, 2018. https://theburgnews.com.
"Our History." Harrisburg Dairies. http://www.harrisburgdairies.com.
Shurtleff, Bertrand Leslie. *AWOL: K-9 Commando*. Amazon. https://www.amazon.com/AWOL-Commando-Bertrand-Leslie-Shurtleff/dp/B0007DPG7W.
*Youth on Trial* (1945). IMDb. https://www.imdb.com.

# ABOUT THE AUTHOR

Rodney J. Ross is a Harrisburg native. He attended Forney Elementary, Edison Junior High School and John Harris High. He is a 1962 Shippensburg State Teachers College graduate. He earned a master's and a doctorate at the Pennsylvania State University. Before retiring in 2017, he taught seven years in the Harrisburg School District and forty-seven at the Harrisburg Area Community College. He has authored academic articles, book reviews and encyclopedia entries. He is researching Harrisburg's experience with World War I and the flu pandemic. He and his wife reside in Lower Paxton Township with their shih tzu, Prince.